WeightWatchers
PointsPlus

TASTIER THAN TAKE⊘UT

ANTIPASTO SUBMARINE
SANDWICHES, PAGE 38

WeightWatchers®
PointsPlus®

TASTIER
THAN
TAKEOUT

RESTAURANT CLASSICS
YOU CAN MAKE AT HOME

PORK AND MUSHROOM MU SHU ROLLS,
PAGE 156; AND HOT-AND-SOUR SOUP WITH
SMOKED TOFU, PAGE 158

ABOUT WeightWatchers®

Weight Watchers International, Inc. is the world's leading provider of weight-management services, operating globally through a network of company-owned and franchise operations. Weight Watchers holds nearly 50,000 weekly meetings worldwide, at which members receive group support and education about healthful eating patterns, behavior modification, and physical activity. Weight-loss and weight-management results vary by individual. We recommend that you attend Weight Watchers meetings to benefit from the supportive environment you find there and follow the comprehensive Weight Watchers program, which includes a food plan, an activity plan, and a behavioral component. In addition, Weight Watchers offers a wide range of products, publications, and programs for people interested in weight loss and weight control. For the Weight Watchers meeting nearest you, call **1-800-651-6000.** For information about bringing Weight Watchers to your workplace, call **1-800-8AT-WORK.**

Also visit us at our Web site, **WeightWatchers.com,** and look for **Weight Watchers Magazine** at your newsstand or in your meeting room.

WEIGHT WATCHERS PUBLISHING GROUP

VP, Editorial Director **Nancy Gagliardi**
Creative Director **Ed Melnitsky**
Photo Director **Deborah Hardt**
Managing Editor **Diane Pavia**
Editorial Assistant **Katerina Gkionis**
Food Editor **Eileen Runyan**
Editor **Alice Thompson**
Recipe Developers **David Bonom,
Terri Grieco Kenny, Lori Longbotham,
Maureen Luchejko, Jackie Plant,
Sarah Reynolds**
Production Manager **Alan Biederman**
Photographer **Hector Sanchez**
Food Stylist **Simon Andrews**
Prop Stylist **Sarah Cave**
Designer **Gary Tooth, Empire Design Studio**

CONTENTS

ABOUT OUR RECIPES

While losing weight isn't only about what you eat, Weight Watchers realizes the critical role it plays in your success and overall good health. That's why our philosophy is to offer great-tasting, easy recipes that are nutritious as well as delicious. We make every attempt to use wholesome ingredients and to ensure that our recipes fall within the recommendations of the U.S. Dietary Guidelines for Americans for a diet that promotes health and reduces the risk for disease. If you have special dietary needs, consult with your health-care professional for advice on a diet that is best for you, then adapt these recipes to meet your specific nutritional needs.

To achieve these good-health goals and get the maximum satisfaction from the foods you eat, we suggest you keep the following information in mind while preparing our recipes:

THE PROGRAM AND GOOD NUTRITION

Recipes in this book have been developed for Weight Watchers members who are following the *PointsPlus*® program. *PointsPlus* values are given for each recipe. They're calculated based on the amount of protein, carbohydrates, fat, and fiber contained in a single serving of a recipe.

● Recipes include approximate nutritional information; they are analyzed for Calories (Cal), Total Fat, Saturated Fat (Sat Fat), Trans Fat, Cholesterol (Chol), Sodium (Sod), Carbohydrates (Carb), Sugar, Dietary Fiber (Fib), Protein (Prot), and Calcium (Calc). The nutritional values are calculated by registered dietitians, using nutrition analysis software.

● Substitutions made to the ingredients will alter the per-serving nutritional information and may affect the *PointsPlus* value.

● Our recipes meet Weight Watchers Good Health Guidelines for eating lean proteins and fiber-rich whole grains, and having at least five servings of vegetables and fruits and two servings of low-fat or fat-free dairy products a day, while limiting your intake of saturated fat, sugar, and sodium.

● Health agencies recommend limiting sodium intake. To stay in line with this recommendation we keep sodium levels in our recipes reasonably low; to boost flavor, we often include fresh herbs or a squeeze of citrus instead of salt. If you don't have to restrict your sodium, feel free to add a touch more salt as desired.

● In the recipes, a green triangle (▲) indicates Weight Watchers® Power Foods.

- FYI serving suggestions have a **PointsPlus** value of **0** unless otherwise stated.

- Recipes that work with the Simply Filling technique are listed on page 244. Find more details about this technique at your meeting.

For additional information about the science behind lasting weight loss and more, please visit **WeightWatchers.com/science.**

All **PointsPlus** values in this book are for one serving.

CALCULATIONS NOT WHAT YOU EXPECTED?

- You might expect some of the **PointsPlus** values in this book to be lower when some of the foods they're made from, such as fruits and vegetables, have no **PointsPlus** values. Most fruits and veggies have no **PointsPlus** values when served as a snack or part of a meal, like a cup of berries with a sandwich. But if these foods are part of a recipe, their fiber and nutrient content are incorporated into the recipe calculations. These nutrients can affect the **PointsPlus** values.

- Alcohol is included in our **PointsPlus** calculations. Because alcohol information is generally not included on nutrition labels, it's not an option to include when using the hand calculator or the online calculator. But since we use alcohol information that we get from our nutritionists you might notice discrepancies between the **PointsPlus** values you see in our recipes, and the values you get using the calculator. The **PointsPlus** values listed for our recipes are the most accurate values.

SHOPPING FOR INGREDIENTS

As you learn to eat healthier and add more Weight Watchers Power Foods to your meals, remember these tips for choosing foods wisely:

Lean Meats and Poultry Purchase lean meats and poultry, and trim them of all visible fat before cooking. When poultry is cooked with the skin on, we recommend removing the skin before eating. Nutritional information for recipes that include meat, poultry, and fish is based on cooked, skinless boneless portions (unless otherwise stated), with the fat trimmed.

Seafood Whenever possible, our recipes call for seafood that is sustainable and deemed the most healthful for human consumption so that your choice of seafood is not only good for the oceans but also good for you. For more information about how to make the best seafood choices and to download a pocket guide, go to **environmentaldefensefund.org** or **montereybayaquarium.org**. For information about mercury levels and seafood go to **WeightWatchers.com.**

Produce For best flavor, maximum nutrient content, and the lowest prices, buy fresh, local produce, such as vegetables, leafy greens, and fruits in season. Rinse them thoroughly before using and keep a supply of cut-up vegetables and fruits in your refrigerator for convenient, healthy snacks.

Whole Grains Explore your market for whole-grain products such as whole wheat and whole-grain breads and pastas, brown rice, bulgur, barley, cornmeal, whole wheat couscous, oats, and quinoa to enjoy with your meals.

PREPARATION AND MEASURING

Read the Recipe Take a couple of minutes to read through the ingredients and directions before you start to prepare a recipe. This will prevent you from discovering midway through that you don't have an important ingredient or that a recipe requires several hours of marinating. And it's also a good idea to assemble all ingredients and utensils within easy reach before you begin a recipe.

Weighing and Measuring The success of any recipe depends on accurate weighing and measuring. The effectiveness of the Weight Watchers program and the accuracy of the nutritional analysis depend on correct measuring as well. Use the following techniques:

● Weigh food such as meat, poultry, and fish on a food scale.

● To measure liquids, use a standard glass or plastic measuring cup placed on a level surface. For amounts less than ¼ cup, use standard measuring spoons.

● To measure dry ingredients, use metal or plastic measuring cups that come in ¼-, ⅓-, ½-, and 1-cup sizes. Fill the appropriate cup and level it with the flat edge of a knife or spatula. For amounts less than ¼ cup, use standard measuring spoons.

BAKED FISH AND CLAMS WITH
CILANTRO-MINT SAUCE, PAGE 217

CHAPTER I

Diner-Style Breakfasts

SMOKED SALMON AND EGG WHITE OMELETTE

MORNING CROQUE MONSIEURS

TEX-MEX EGGS MIGAS WITH CHEDDAR AND JALAPEÑO

EGG AND ASPARAGUS BREAKFAST PITAS

ENGLISH MUFFIN BLT WITH AVOCADO

STRAWBERRY ELVIS BREAKFAST SANDWICHES

MINI BAGELS WITH SILKY TOFU-CHERRY SPREAD

WHOLE WHEAT SKILLET PANCAKE WITH PEARS
AND WALNUTS

RICOTTA PANCAKES WITH BERRIES

GET-YOUR-GREENS BREAKFAST SMOOTHIE

FRUIT AND COTTAGE CHEESE SALAD
WITH RASPBERRY-BASIL SAUCE

FRUIT AND FLAX MUESLI MIX

Breakfast Pantry Partners

KEEP THESE STAPLES ON HAND TO MAKE
HEALTHFUL BREAKFASTS A SNAP.

Egg Whites ▲ Cartons of pasteurized egg whites are available in the dairy section of most supermarkets, and they're super convenient for making lower-fat omelets, scrambles, and baked goods. Use 2 tablespoons of pasteurized egg whites in place of the separated white of one large egg.

Frozen Berries ▲ Keep a bag of frozen unsweetened berries in the freezer to add great taste and nutrition to everything from yogurt to pancakes and oatmeal. You can substitute frozen for fresh berries in most recipes, and if you're adding them to muffins or smoothies, you won't even have to thaw them first.

Hard-Cooked Eggs ▲ Protein- and nutrient-rich hard-cooked eggs are ultrahandy for breakfasts on the go. You can slice or dice them for adding to sandwiches or salads, or eat them whole with a pinch of salt or a dollop of mustard. They keep refrigerated in the shell up to 1 week.

Mini Whole Wheat Bagels Chewy, flavorful whole wheat minis have become a favorite with bagel lovers of all ages. Use them for making easy breakfast sandwiches, or tote them to the office with your favorite low-fat spread.

Plain Soy Milk Shake up your dairy routine by trying out nutty, healthful soy milk. It's excellent in smoothies and over morning cereal.

Quick-Cooking Oats You know they're great for a quick bowl of hot whole-grain cereal, but you can also use quick oats as the base for delicious (and economical) homemade muesli or granola.

Reduced-Calorie Sandwich Bread ▲ This is a top choice for toast, and excellent for quick breakfast sandwiches as well. Choose whole wheat or multigrain for best nutrition.

Turkey Bacon Not only is turkey bacon lower in fat than standard pork bacon, it also cooks up a bit more quickly and with much less splattering. Want to save even more time in the morning? Look for fully cooked, ready-to-eat turkey bacon at your supermarket.

Wheat Bran ▲ Made from the outermost layer of wheat kernels, wheat bran is an excellent source of natural fiber. It's ideal for adding to hot or cold cereal or sprinkling over cottage cheese or yogurt.

SMOKED SALMON AND EGG WHITE OMELETTE

SERVES 1 • READY IN 20 MIN OR LESS

▲ **4   large egg whites**

1   tablespoon water

▲ **1   scallion, chopped**

⅛   teaspoon black pepper

1   teaspoon unsalted butter

1   ounce (about 3 slices) smoked salmon

▲ **1   tablespoon fat-free sour cream**

1   teaspoon drained capers, chopped

Chopped fresh dill

① Whisk egg whites and water in medium bowl until frothy. Whisk in scallion and pepper.

② Melt butter in small nonstick skillet over medium heat, swirling butter to coat pan. Pour in egg mixture and cook, stirring gently, until underside is set, 1–2 minutes. Top one half of omelet with salmon, sour cream, and capers; fold other half over filling. Cook until eggs are set, 1–2 minutes. Slide omelette onto plate and sprinkle with dill.

PER SERVING (1 omelette): 148 Cal, 5 g Total Fat, 3 g Sat Fat, 0 g Trans Fat, 18 mg Chol, 393 mg Sod, 5 g Carb, 1 g Sugar, 1 g Fib, 20 g Prot, 47 mg Calc.

FYI

Serve this light and delicious omelette with 2 slices of toasted reduced-calorie whole wheat bread for an additional *2 PointsPlus* value.

MORNING CROQUE MONSIEURS

SERVES 2 • READY IN 20 MIN OR LESS

▲ **4** slices reduced-calorie multi-grain bread

▲ **4** (¾-ounce) slices lean roasted lower-sodium deli-sliced ham

▲ **2** (¾-ounce) slices fat-free Swiss cheese

▲ **1** small tomato, sliced

8 basil leaves (optional)

▲ **1** large egg

▲ **2** tablespoons fat-free milk

1 teaspoon Dijon mustard

❶ Place 2 slices bread on work surface; top each with 2 slices ham, 1 slice Swiss cheese, a few tomato slices, and 4 basil leaves (if using). Cover each sandwich with slice of remaining bread. Whisk egg, milk, and mustard in large bowl until frothy.

❷ Spray large nonstick skillet with nonstick spray and set over medium heat. Working one sandwich at a time, dip both sides into egg mixture, and then place in skillet. Cook sandwiches until undersides are browned, about 3 minutes. Turn sandwiches over, cover skillet, and cook until heated through, about 3 minutes longer.

PER SERVING (1 sandwich): 263 Cal, 7 g Total Fat, 2 g Sat Fat, 2 g Trans Fat, 135 mg Chol, 957 mg Sod, 34 g Carb, 5 g Sugar, 11 g Fib, 24 g Prot, 313 mg Calc.

7
PointsPlus®
value

TEX-MEX EGGS MIGAS WITH CHEDDAR AND JALAPEÑO

SERVES 4 • READY IN 20 MIN OR LESS

▲ 5 **large egg whites**

▲ 3 **large eggs**

Pinch salt

1 **tablespoon water**

2 **teaspoons canola oil**

4 **(6-inch) corn tortillas, cut into thin strips**

▲ 1 **onion, diced**

▲ ½ **jalapeño pepper, seeded and finely chopped**

▲ 1 **cup shredded fat-free Cheddar cheese**

▲ 6 **tablespoons prepared fat-free chunky salsa**

▲ 8 **teaspoons fat-free sour cream**

❶ Whisk egg whites, eggs, salt, and water in medium bowl until frothy.

❷ Heat oil in large nonstick skillet over medium-high heat. Add tortilla strips and cook, stirring often, until they begin to brown, 1–2 minutes. Stir in onion and jalapeño and cook until softened, 3–4 minutes. Pour in eggs and cook, stirring frequently, until almost set, about 2 minutes. Stir in Cheddar cheese and cook until melted, about 45 seconds. Divide mixture among 4 plates; top each serving with 1 ½ tablespoons salsa and 2 teaspoons sour cream.

PER SERVING (¾ cup eggs, 1½ tablespoons salsa, and 2 teaspoons sour cream): 251 Cal, 7 g Total Fat, 1 g Sat Fat, 0 g Trans Fat, 16 mg Chol, 486 mg Sod, 27 g Carb, 3 g Sugar, 2 g Fib, 20 g Prot, 318 mg Calc.

EGG AND ASPARAGUS BREAKFAST PITAS

SERVES 2 • READY IN 20 MIN OR LESS

▲ **2 large hard-cooked eggs, chopped**

▲ **2 large hard-cooked egg whites, chopped**

2 teaspoons fat-free mayonnaise

▲ **2 teaspoons plain fat-free yogurt**

Pinch salt

Pinch black pepper

2 (2-ounce) whole-grain pitas

▲ **10 spears steamed asparagus, chopped**

▲ **1 cup radish or other sprouts**

Stir together eggs, egg whites, mayonnaise, yogurt, salt, and pepper in small bowl. Cut top third off each pita and discard, or save to make bread crumbs. Stuff pitas evenly with egg mixture, asparagus, and sprouts. Serve immediately, or wrap in plastic and refrigerate up to 2 days.

PER SERVING (1 filled pita): 229 Cal, 7 g Total Fat, 2 g Sat Fat, 0 g Trans Fat, 213 mg Chol, 436 mg Sod, 27 g Carb, 4 g Sugar, 5 g Fib, 17 g Prot, 73 mg Calc.

6 PointsPlus® value

Diner Breakfasts

FYI

Complement this sandwich with a side of refreshing fruit. Try it with sweet-tart pink grapefruit or, if you need something convenient to tote to the office, try a container of mixed fruit cocktail packed in water.

ENGLISH MUFFIN BLT WITH AVOCADO

SERVES 4 • READY IN 20 MIN OR LESS

4   slices turkey bacon

3   tablespoons fat-free mayonnaise

½   teaspoon grated lemon zest

½   teaspoon hot pepper sauce, or to taste

4   multi-grain English muffins, split and toasted

▲ 4   small Boston lettuce leaves

½   Hass avocado, cut into 12 slices

▲ 4   slices tomato

① Spray medium nonstick skillet with nonstick spray and set over medium heat. Add bacon and cook, turning once, until crisp, 5–7 minutes. Transfer to cutting board; cut each slice in half crosswise.

② Meanwhile, combine mayonnaise, zest, and pepper sauce in small bowl. Spread inside of each muffin with about 2 teaspoons mayonnaise mixture and fill each with 1 lettuce leaf, 3 avocado slices, 1 tomato slice, and 2 pieces bacon. Serve immediately, or wrap in plastic and refrigerate up to 2 days.

PER SERVING (1 sandwich): 243 Cal, 9 g Total Fat, 2 g Sat Fat, 0 g Trans Fat, 15 mg Chol, 745 mg Sod, 32 g Carb, 7 g Sugar, 7 g Fib, 11 g Prot, 183 mg Calc.

FYI

If you're not eating these tasty breakfast muffins immediately, you may want to toss the avocado slices with a teaspoon of lemon juice before adding them to the sandwiches; the juice will help prevent the avocado from browning.

STRAWBERRY ELVIS BREAKFAST SANDWICHES

SERVES 4 • READY IN 20 MIN OR LESS

▲ 6   strawberries, hulled and sliced

1   teaspoon sugar

1   tablespoon water

½   teaspoon fresh lemon juice

▲ 8   slices reduced-calorie multi-grain bread, toasted

4   tablespoons reduced-fat creamy peanut butter

▲ 2   medium bananas, sliced

1 Combine strawberries, sugar, and water in small nonstick skillet over medium heat. Cook, stirring, until strawberries soften, 2–3 minutes. Remove from heat and stir in lemon juice.

2 Meanwhile, spread one side of 4 slices bread with 1 tablespoon peanut butter. Top each with one fourth of strawberry slices and one fourth of banana slices. Cover sandwiches with remaining 4 slices bread. Cut each sandwich in half on an angle. Serve immediately, or wrap in plastic and refrigerate up to 2 days.

PER SERVING (1 sandwich): 236 Cal, 7 g Total Fat, 1 g Sat Fat, 0 g Trans Fat, 0 mg Chol, 366 mg Sod, 43 g Carb, 14 g Sugar, 9 g Fib, 9 g Prot, 46 mg Calc.

FYI

Elvis Presley was known for craving peanut butter and banana sandwiches any time of the day or night, so we're pretty sure he would have approved of this breakfast version. Our quick homemade strawberry compote gives the sandwich a little extra distinction, but you can use 1 tablespoon strawberry fruit spread instead on each sandwich for no extra *PointsPlus* value.

MINI BAGELS WITH SILKY TOFU-CHERRY SPREAD

SERVES 6 • READY IN 20 MIN OR LESS

▲ ½ **(14-ounce) package extra-firm silken tofu, drained**

▲ 1 **cup frozen thawed unsweetened cherries, drained**

2 **teaspoons honey**

1½ **teaspoons lemon juice**

Few drops almond extract (optional)

6 **mini whole wheat bagels, split**

❶ Place tofu on plate lined with paper towels. Set another plate on top to weight it. Let stand 10 minutes to remove excess liquid. Drain and discard liquid.

❷ Puree tofu, cherries, honey, lemon juice, and almond extract (if using) in food processor. Toast bagels just before serving and spread each with ¼ cup of tofu mixture.

PER SERVING (1 mini bagel and ¼ cup tofu spread):
104 Cal, 1 g Total Fat, 0 g Sat Fat, 0 g Trans Fat,
0 mg Chol, 153 mg Sod, 19 g Carb, 5 g Sugar, 1 g Fib,
5 g Prot, 17 mg Calc.

3 PointsPlus® value

WHOLE WHEAT SKILLET PANCAKE
WITH PEARS AND WALNUTS

WHOLE WHEAT SKILLET PANCAKE WITH PEARS AND WALNUTS

SERVES 6

- ▲ 2 **large eggs**
- ▲ 2 **large egg whites**
- ▲ 1 **cup fat-free milk**
-    1 **tablespoon brown sugar**
-    ½ **teaspoon cinnamon**
-    ¼ **teaspoon salt**
-    ¾ **cup whole wheat pastry flour**
- ▲ 2 **Bartlett pears, cored and thinly sliced**
-    2 **tablespoons finely chopped walnuts**
-    2 **teaspoons confectioners' sugar**

① Preheat oven to 425°F. Place large (11- or 12-inch) cast-iron or ovenproof skillet in oven to heat up.

② Meanwhile, combine eggs, egg whites, milk, brown sugar, cinnamon, and salt in blender and blend until smooth. Add flour and pulse just until combined. Wearing oven mitt, remove skillet from oven and spray with nonstick spray. Pour in batter. Top with pears and sprinkle with walnuts. Bake until pancake is puffed and browned and pears are softened, 15–20 minutes. Sprinkle with confectioners' sugar and cut into 6 wedges.

PER SERVING (1 wedge): 160 Cal, 3 g Total Fat, 1 g Sat Fat, 0 g Trans Fat, 72 mg Chol, 155 mg Sod, 27 g Carb, 11 g Sugar, 4 g Fib, 7 g Prot, 80 mg Calc.

FYI

After baking, top your pancake with a fruit garnish if you like. Sliced plums, blueberries, or raspberries are delicious choices.

RICOTTA PANCAKES WITH BERRIES

SERVES 4 • READY IN 20 MIN OR LESS

⅔ **cup whole wheat pastry flour**

1 **tablespoon sugar**

1 **teaspoon baking powder**

½ **teaspoon ground ginger**

¼ **teaspoon salt**

▲ 1 **cup fat-free ricotta cheese**

▲ 1 **large egg**

▲ 1 **large egg white**

▲ ¾ **cup fat-free milk**

¾ **teaspoon vanilla extract**

▲ 2 **cups mixed berries**

1 Whisk flour, sugar, baking powder, ginger, and salt together in medium bowl. Whisk ricotta, egg, egg white, milk, and vanilla together in large bowl. Add dry ingredients to wet ingredients, stirring just until blended.

2 Spray large nonstick skillet or griddle with nonstick spray and set over medium heat. When hot, drop batter by ¼ cupfuls onto pan (work in batches if necessary to avoid crowding pan). Cook each until underside is browned and bubbles begin to form on top, 3–4 minutes. Flip pancakes and cook other sides. Repeat with remaining batter, making 8 pancakes. Serve with berries.

PER SERVING (2 pancakes and ½ cup berries):
201 Cal, 2 g Total Fat, 0 g Sat Fat, 0 g Trans Fat, 60 mg Chol, 413 mg Sod, 32 g Carb, 12 g Sugar, 4 g Fib, 14 g Prot, 309 mg Calc.

OURS vs. THEIRS

Putting breakfast together at home not only saves money, it also makes it easy to choose smarter, healthier foods. Here are a few examples of how recipes in this chapter stack up against common takeout options, plus some suggestions for satisfying foods you can enjoy with the savings.

YOUR CHOICE	OURS	THEIRS	WITH YOUR SAVINGS TRY
OMELETTE	Our Smoked Salmon and Egg White Omelette, p. 16: **4 *PointsPlus*** value	2-egg diner-style vegetable omelette: **8 *PointsPlus*** value	⅔ cup low-fat vanilla yogurt: **4 *PointsPlus*** value
CROQUE MONSIEUR	One of our Morning Croque Monsieurs, p. 17: **7 *PointsPlus*** value	6½-ounce bistro-style croque monsieur: **12 *PointsPlus*** value	⅔ cup of orange juice and a latte made with 1½ cups fat-free milk and no sugar: **5 *PointsPlus*** value total
ENGLISH MUFFIN SANDWICH	One of our English Muffin BLT with Avocado sandwiches, p. 20: **6 *PointsPlus*** value	A 4¾-ounce fast food–style egg, cheese, and Canadian bacon muffin: **8 *PointsPlus*** value	1 large hard-cooked egg: **2 *PointsPlus*** value
BAGEL	One of our Mini Bagels with Silky Tofu-Cherry Spread, p. 23: **3 *PointsPlus*** value	½ large bagel spread with 1 tablespoon cream cheese: **5 *PointsPlus*** value	⅔ cup carrot juice: **2 *PointsPlus*** value
PANCAKES	Two of our Ricotta Pancakes with Berries, p. 26: **5 *PointsPlus*** value	Two fast-food pancakes with butter and syrup: **14 *PointsPlus*** value	Get-Your-Greens Breakfast Smoothie, p. 28, and 2 plain rice cakes: **9 *PointsPlus*** value total

GET-YOUR-GREENS BREAKFAST SMOOTHIE

SERVES 1 • READY IN 20 MIN OR LESS

¾   **cup (6 ounces) vanilla soy yogurt**

½   **cup plain soy milk**

▲ 2   **cups baby spinach leaves**

▲ ½   **small banana**

¼   **teaspoon vanilla extract**

5   **ice cubes**

Combine all ingredients in blender and puree. Pour into tall glass.

PER SERVING (1½ cups): 278 Cal, 6 g Total Fat, 1 g Sat Fat, 0 g Trans Fat, 0 mg Chol, 104 mg Sod, 44 g Carb, 25 g Sugar, 5 g Fib, 13 g Prot, 384 mg Calc.

FYI

If you like, go even greener by adding a peeled kiwi to the ingredients.

GET-YOUR-GREENS BREAKFAST
SMOOTHIE AND FRUIT AND FLAX
MUESLI MIX, PAGE 31

FRUIT AND COTTAGE CHEESE SALAD WITH RASPBERRY-BASIL SAUCE

SERVES 4 • READY IN 20 MIN OR LESS

▲ 2 cups cubed watermelon

▲ 2 cups cubed cantaloupe

▲ 2 cups cubed honeydew

▲ 1 medium mango, peeled, pitted, and cut into ½-inch cubes

▲ 1 pint fresh blueberries, rinsed and drained

¼ cup seedless raspberry fruit spread

3 tablespoons chopped fresh basil leaves

Juice and zest of ½ lemon

▲ 2 cups fat-free cottage cheese

① Combine watermelon, cantaloupe, honeydew, mango, and blueberries in large bowl.

② Place fruit spread in a small microwavable bowl; microwave on High until warmed and slightly melted, 20 to 30 seconds. Stir in basil and lemon juice and zest. Pour raspberry mixture over fruit and toss to coat. Divide among 4 bowls and top each serving with ½ cup cottage cheese.

PER SERVING (2 cups fruit, 2 tablespoons sauce, and ½ cup cottage cheese): 284 Cal, 1 g Total Fat, 0 g Sat Fat, 0 g Trans Fat, 5 mg Chol, 461 mg Sod, 58 g Carb, 48 g Sugar, 5 g Fib, 16 g Prot, 92 mg Calc.

8 PointsPlus® value

FRUIT AND FLAX MUESLI MIX

SERVES 12 • READY IN 20 MIN OR LESS

3   **cups quick-cooking oats**

¾   **cup ground flaxseed**

¾   **cup golden raisins**

¾   **cup dried cherries**

½   **cup sliced almonds**

½   **cup raw green pumpkin seeds**

3   **tablespoons wheat bran**

2   **tablespoons brown sugar**

1½   **teaspoons cinnamon**

Combine all ingredients in large bowl and toss to mix. Store in airtight container up to 3 weeks.

PER SERVING (½ cup): 252 Cal, 8 g Total Fat, 1 g Sat Fat, 0 g Trans Fat, 0 mg Chol, 6 mg Sod, 37 g Carb, 15 g Sugar, 8 g Fib, 9 g Prot, 41 mg Calc.

FYI

You can eat this delicious breakfast cereal hot or cold. To heat it, combine ½ cup muesli with ½ cup water in a microwavable bowl and microwave on High until oats are softened and cereal just bubbles around the edge, 1–2 minutes. Try it topped with fruit.

COFFEE & ESPRE

HOT

COFFEE	1.00
TEA	.75
ESPRESSO	1.50
LATTE	2.50
CAPPUCCINO	2.25
MACCHIATO	1.00
MOCHACCINO	3.00
CHAI LATTE	2.25

DELI

Scones	Basil & Black pepper
- Blueberry	BISCUIT
- Cranberry	w/ Vermont cultured butter
- Chocolate Chip	
$2	$1.50

& ROASTED MEATS
IN-HOUSE!!

* ALL ORGANIC

SANDWICHES MAKE YOUR OWN!!

COFFEE & ESPRESSO

BREAD	MEAT	CHEESE	TOPPINGS
	ST BEEF 2.	SWISS	LETTUCE
	M 6.	BLUE	TOM
	MI 7	MOZZ	
	F 7 GOAT		
		WH. CHED	

BULK TEAS AVAILABLE

	HOT		**ICED**	
	SM.	LARGE	SM	LARGE
COFFEE		2.00	1.75	2.00
	.75	2.25	1.50	2.00
	1.50			
	2.50	3.25		3.75
	2.30	3.25		
	3.25	4.	3.75	4.50
	2.50	2.75		
	3.00	3.75		3.75

ESPRESSO SHOTS 1.
OR SHOTS .50

AILABLE WHOLE B
FRESHLY GROUND

NATURAL
CAPE COD
CRANBERRY MIX

APPLE RINGS

CLOSED

ORGANIC

CHAPTER 2

Deli-Delicious Lunches

CURRIED BEEF AND MANGO WRAPS

SANTA FE CHICKEN PANINIS

ANTIPASTO SUBMARINE SANDWICHES

ZESTY PIZZA ROLL-UP

SPICY TUNA SALAD ROLLS

GREEN CHILE AND CHEDDAR TURKEY BURGERS

LOADED VEGGIE SANDWICHES

TURKEY AND BLACK BEAN CHILI SOUP

SAUSAGE, WHITE BEAN, AND SWEET POTATO SOUP

SALMON AND CORN CHOWDER

SPICY TORTELLINI AND ROAST TOMATO SOUP

SMOKED CHICKEN WALDORF SALAD

TURKEY NACHO SALAD

SALMON PASTA SALAD WITH SUGAR SNAPS AND DILL

TUNA AND NEW POTATO SALAD WITH BASIL DRESSING

Lunch Pantry Partners

KEEP THESE STAPLES ON HAND TO MAKE HEALTHFUL LUNCHES A SNAP.

Canned Beans ▲ Protein-rich, fiber-rich beans are a healthful and economical addition to soups and salads. No-salt-added canned beans are readily available and an easy way to reduce the sodium in bean recipes.

Canned Water-Packed Salmon and Tuna ▲ Fish packed in water (not oil) is ideal for adding to salads, sandwiches, and wraps. Both salmon and tuna are loaded with protein and heart-healthy omega-3s.

Fat-Free Cheeses ▲ These are super convenient stars for salads and sandwiches, and they're also a satisfying afternoon snack to have with a piece of fruit.

Hummus Not only is it a great dip, hummus also makes a delicious, protein-packed sandwich spread. Need variety? Try a flavored hummus like garlic, roasted red pepper, or tomato-basil.

Packaged Greens ▲ Fresh, prewashed greens come in more varieties than ever, and they're indispensable for putting together salads and sandwiches on the fly. They're great for soups too—look for baby spinach and baby kale to add quick taste and texture.

Reduced-Calorie Sandwich Bread ▲ This is a convenient, healthful choice for sandwiches and a good accompaniment for soups and salads. Choose whole wheat or multigrain breads for best nutrition.

Reduced-Sodium Broths ▲ Keep a few cans or cartons of your favorite broths on hand for putting together quick, satisfying soups.

Roasted Red Bell Peppers ▲ Bell peppers roasted and packed in water (not oil) make a quick, colorful, naturally sweet addition for salads and sandwiches.

Sandwich Thins A.k.a. flat rolls, you can find these in the bread section of your supermarket. These very thin, split flat breads give good bread flavor and texture without overwhelming your sandwich filling. Choose whole-grain varieties for best nutrition.

Whole Wheat and Multigrain Tortillas Keep tortillas (8- or 10-inch) on hand, and you can roll your own lunch wraps at a moment's notice. Slice wraps crosswise into small pieces like pinwheels for a festive change.

Deli-Delicious Lunches

CURRIED BEEF AND MANGO WRAPS

SERVES 2 • READY IN 20 MIN OR LESS

2 tablespoons fat-free mayonnaise

1 tablespoon mango chutney, chopped

1 teaspoon grated lime zest

½ teaspoon curry powder

2 (8-inch) lower-sodium multigrain tortillas

▲ 2 Boston lettuce leaves

▲ 2 (1-ounce) slices lean thinly sliced sirloin roast beef

▲ ½ red bell pepper, thinly sliced

▲ ½ mango, thinly sliced

1 Combine mayonnaise, chutney, lime zest, and curry powder in small bowl.

2 Place tortillas on work surface and spread evenly with mayonnaise mixture. Top each with 1 lettuce leaf and 1 slice roast beef. Arrange bell pepper and mango on bottom third of tortillas. Roll up tortillas and cut in half.

PER SERVING (1 wrap): 224 Cal, 7 g Total Fat, 1 g Sat Fat, 0 g Trans Fat, 26 mg Chol, 595 mg Sod, 35 g Carb, 11 g Sugar, 15 g Fib, 18 g Prot, 21 mg Calc.

SANTA FE CHICKEN PANINIS

SERVES 2 • READY IN 20 MIN OR LESS

2   whole wheat sandwich thins

4   teaspoons chipotle mustard

▲ 1   cup (¼ pound) shredded cooked skinless boneless chicken breast

▲ ½   red bell pepper, thinly sliced

2   ounces reduced-fat lower-sodium pepper Jack cheese, thinly sliced

❶ Preheat panini press or large nonstick skillet over medium heat.

❷ Spread each sandwich thin with mustard and evenly fill with chicken, bell pepper, and pepper Jack. Lightly spray top and bottom of each sandwich with nonstick spray and place in pan. Cook until bread is toasted and cheese melts, about 8 minutes, turning once if using skillet. Slice sandwiches in half and serve.

PER SERVING (1 panini): 291 Cal, 8 g Total Fat, 3 g Sat Fat, 0 g Trans Fat, 70 mg Chol, 483 mg Sod, 23 g Carb, 3 g Sugar, 7 g Fib, 32 g Prot, 163 mg Calc.

7 PointsPlus® value ™

FYI

If you like, serve a side of fat-free salsa and carrot sticks with these sandwiches. If you don't have chipotle mustard, substitute regular mustard mixed with a few drops of hot pepper sauce.

Deli-Delicious Lunches

ANTIPASTO SUBMARINE SANDWICHES

SERVES 4 • READY IN 20 MIN OR LESS

¾ cup shredded unsalted mozzarella cheese

▲ 1 celery stalk, thinly sliced

▲ ¼ cup roasted red bell pepper (not oil-packed), chopped

▲ 2 pepperoncini peppers, stemmed, seeded, and thinly sliced

4 small pimiento-stuffed green olives, chopped

2 teaspoons red wine vinegar

1 teaspoon olive oil

¼ teaspoon Italian seasoning blend

1 (8-ounce) whole wheat baguette, cut in half horizontally

▲ 4 ounces thinly sliced lean baked lower-sodium ham

▲ 2 plum tomatoes, sliced

▲ 4 romaine lettuce leaves, thinly sliced

1 Toss mozzarella, celery, roasted bell pepper, pepperoncini, olives, vinegar, oil, and Italian seasoning in medium bowl.

2 Remove small amount of soft center from baguette and discard, or save for bread crumbs. Layer ham, cheese mixture, tomatoes, and lettuce on bottom of baguette. Cover with top; slice into 4 sandwiches. Serve immediately, or wrap in plastic and refrigerate up to 1 day.

PER SERVING (1 sandwich): 292 Cal, 9 g Total Fat, 3 g Sat Fat, 0 g Trans Fat, 26 mg Chol, 969 mg Sod, 35 g Carb, 4 g Sugar, 5 g Fib, 19 g Prot, 187 mg Calc.

FYI

Instead of mixing the olives into the sandwich filling, you can spear each on a toothpick and use them to hold the sandwiches together.

ZESTY PIZZA ROLL-UP

SERVES 1 • READY IN 20 MIN OR LESS

▲ **1** cup sliced cremini mushrooms

1 (8-inch) low-sodium whole-grain tortilla

2 tablespoons pizza sauce

¼ cup shredded unsalted mozzarella cheese

4 thin slices turkey pepperoni, halved

▲ **½** cup lightly packed baby spinach leaves

❶ Place mushrooms on microwavable plate. Microwave on High until tender, about 2 minutes. Blot with paper towels to remove moisture. Transfer mushrooms to small bowl.

❷ Place tortilla on plate covered with paper towel. Spread tortilla with pizza sauce to ¼ inch from edge. Sprinkle with mozzarella and top with pepperoni. Microwave on High until cheese melts, about 1 minute. Top with spinach and mushrooms; microwave on High until mushrooms are hot, about 20 seconds. Roll up and cut in half.

PER SERVING (1 roll up): 209 Cal, 9 g Total Fat, 3 g Sat Fat, 0 g Trans Fat, 24 mg Chol, 591 mg Sod, 22 g Carb, 3 g Sugar, 11 g Fib, 19 g Prot, 230 mg Calc.

FYI

Serve this tasty roll-up with a colorful salad of mixed Italian greens, sliced red bell pepper, and grated carrot tossed with balsamic vinegar.

SPICY TUNA SALAD ROLLS

SERVES 2 • READY IN 20 MIN OR LESS

▲ 1 (5-ounce) can no-salt-added water-packed light tuna, drained

2 tablespoons fat-free mayonnaise

▲ 1 scallion, chopped

1 teaspoon Sriracha (hot chili sauce) or other hot sauce

2 (8-inch) lower-sodium whole wheat tortillas

▲ ½ cup cooked and cooled brown rice

▲ ½ cucumber, peeled, seeded, and cut into thin strips

▲ 1 small carrot, cut into thin strips

▲ 1 cup lightly packed baby spinach leaves

1 tablespoon sliced pickled ginger, finely chopped

2 teaspoons rice vinegar

1 teaspoon reduced-sodium soy sauce

2 teaspoons water

❶ Mix together tuna, mayonnaise, scallion, and Sriracha in small bowl.

❷ Place tortillas on work surface and spread evenly with tuna mixture. Evenly divide rice, cucumber, carrot, and spinach between tortillas, placing on bottom third in strips. Roll tortillas up tightly. Trim ends and cut each roll into 4 pieces.

❸ Mix ginger, vinegar, soy sauce, and water in small bowl. Serve as dipping sauce with rolls.

PER SERVING (4 pieces roll and 1 tablespoon dipping sauce): 336 Cal, 6 g Total Fat, 2 g Sat Fat, 0 g Trans Fat, 23 mg Chol, 862 mg Sod, 45 g Carb, 7 g Sugar, 8 g Fib, 25 g Prot, 147 mg Calc.

8 PointsPlus® value

GREEN CHILE AND CHEDDAR
TURKEY BURGERS

GREEN CHILE AND CHEDDAR TURKEY BURGERS

SERVES 4

- ▲ 1 pound ground skinless turkey breast
- ▲ 1 small zucchini, shredded
- ⅓ cup dried whole wheat bread crumbs
- 1 teaspoon chili powder
- ½ teaspoon ground cumin
- ▲ 1 (4-ounce) can diced fire-roasted green chiles, drained
- ▲ ⅓ cup shredded fat-free Cheddar cheese
- ▲ ½ small red onion, thinly sliced
- ▲ 1 tomato, sliced
- 4 whole wheat sandwich thins

❶ Combine turkey, zucchini, bread crumbs, chili powder, and cumin in large bowl. Shape into 4 (¾-inch-thick) patties.

❷ Spray nonstick skillet with nonstick spray and set over medium heat. Add patties and cook until browned and instant-read thermometer inserted into side of patties registers 165°F, 4–5 minutes per side.

❸ Meanwhile, mix chiles and Cheddar in medium bowl.

❹ Top burgers evenly with cheese mixture. Reduce heat to low; cover skillet and cook until cheese melts, about 2 minutes. Serve burgers, onion, and tomato in sandwich thins.

PER SERVING (1 burger): 298 Cal, 3 g Total Fat, 0 g Sat Fat, 0 g Trans Fat, 47 mg Chol, 594 mg Sod, 32 g Carb, 5 g Sugar, 8 g Fib, 38 g Prot, 132 mg Calc.

FYI

Canned fire-roasted green chiles are very mild; if you like things spicy, add some chopped seeded jalapeño pepper.

x

x

Deli-Delicious Lunches

LOADED VEGGIE SANDWICHES

SERVES 2 • READY IN 20 MIN OR LESS

▲ **4** slices reduced-calorie
whole-grain bread

¼ cup tomato-basil hummus

2 teaspoons Dijon mustard

▲ **1** carrot, shredded

▲ **½** cucumber, peeled and thinly sliced

2 (¾-ounce) slices reduced-sodium
low-fat Swiss cheese

▲ **1** tomato, sliced

▲ **2** red lettuce leaves

Place bread slices on work surface. Spread 2 slices with hummus and remaining 2 slices with mustard. Evenly divide carrot, cucumber, cheese, tomato, and lettuce between hummus-topped slices. Cover with remaining bread slices. Cut sandwiches in half. Serve immediately, or wrap in plastic and refrigerate up to 2 days.

PER SERVING (1 sandwich): 243 Cal, 8 g Total Fat, 3 g Sat Fat, 0 g Trans Fat, 15 mg Chol, 479 mg Sod, 30 g Carb, 6 g Sugar, 5 g Fib, 14 g Prot, 263 mg Calc.

FYI

If you like, add a ¼ cup of crunchy watercress sprigs or pea sprouts to each sandwich in addition to the lettuce.

TURKEY AND BLACK BEAN CHILI SOUP

SERVES 4

▲ ¾ pound ground skinless turkey breast

▲ 1 small onion, finely chopped

3 garlic cloves, minced

1 tablespoon chili powder

1 teaspoon ground cumin

▲ 2½ cups reduced-sodium chicken broth

▲ 1 (15-ounce) can no-salt-added diced tomatoes

▲ 1 (15-ounce) can reduced-sodium black beans, rinsed and drained

▲ ¼ cup quick-cooking brown rice

▲ 1 zucchini, diced

▲ 1 summer squash, diced

▲ 8 tablespoons shredded fat-free Cheddar cheese

1 Spray large saucepan with nonstick spray and set over medium-high heat. Add turkey and onion. Cook, stirring frequently and breaking up turkey with side of spoon, until turkey is no longer pink, about 4 minutes. Stir in garlic, chili powder, and cumin. Add broth and tomatoes. Bring to boil and stir in beans and rice. Reduce heat; cover and simmer until rice is tender, about 10 minutes.

2 Stir in zucchini and summer squash. Bring to boil. Reduce heat; cover and simmer until vegetables are tender, about 8 minutes. Divide among 4 bowls and sprinkle each serving with 2 tablespoons cheese.

PER SERVING (1½ cups soup and 2 tablespoons cheese): 276 Cal, 3 g Total Fat, 0 g Sat Fat, 0 g Trans Fat, 36 mg Chol, 451 mg Sod, 33 g Carb, 7 g Sugar, 9 g Fib, 36 g Prot, 218 mg Calc.

7 PointsPlus® value

Deli-Delicious Lunches

SAUSAGE, WHITE BEAN, AND SWEET POTATO SOUP

SERVES 4

- ▲ 1 small onion, finely chopped
- ▲ 3 cups reduced-sodium chicken broth
- ▲ 1 (8-ounce) sweet potato, peeled and shredded
- ▲ 1 large tomato, coarsely chopped
- 2 large garlic cloves, minced
- ½ pound fully cooked chicken sausages, sliced
- ▲ 1 (15-ounce) can no-salt-added cannellini beans, rinsed and drained
- ▲ 1 (6-ounce) bag baby spinach leaves
- 4 teaspoons shaved Parmesan cheese

❶ Spray large saucepan with olive oil nonstick spray and set over medium heat. Add onion and cook, stirring occasionally, until softened, about 3 minutes. Add broth, sweet potato, tomato, and garlic. Bring to boil over high heat. Stir in sausage and beans. Reduce heat to medium-low; cover and simmer until vegetables are tender, about 10 minutes.

❷ Stir in spinach; cover and simmer until spinach wilts, about 2 minutes. Divide soup among 4 bowls and sprinkle with cheese.

PER SERVING (1¾ cups soup and 1 teaspoon cheese): 289 Cal, 7 g Total Fat, 2 g Sat Fat, 0 g Trans Fat, 45 mg Chol, 534 mg Sod, 37 g Carb, 5 g Sugar, 9 g Fib, 22 g Prot, 116 mg Calc.

7 PointsPlus® value

FYI

To vary the flavors in this soup, use black beans in place of cannellini, and add ½ teaspoon chipotle chile powder along with the garlic in Step 1.

SAUSAGE, WHITE BEAN,
AND SWEET POTATO SOUP

SALMON AND CORN CHOWDER

SERVES 4

▲ 1   onion, finely chopped

   4   slices Canadian bacon, diced

▲ 3   cups reduced-sodium chicken broth

▲ 2   small red potatoes, diced

▲ 1   cup frozen baby lima beans

   ¼   teaspoon dried thyme

   ¼   teaspoon salt

   ¼   teaspoon black pepper

▲ 1½ cups thawed frozen corn kernels

▲ ⅓   cup fat-free half-and-half

▲ ½   pound skinless wild salmon fillet,
       cut into 1-inch chunks

❶ Spray large saucepan with nonstick spray and set over medium-high heat. Add onion and bacon. Cook, stirring frequently, until lightly browned, 3–4 minutes. Add broth, potatoes, lima beans, thyme, salt, and pepper. Bring to boil. Reduce heat; cover and simmer until potatoes are tender, about 10 minutes.

❷ Meanwhile, combine ½ cup corn with half-and-half in blender and puree.

❸ Stir salmon and whole corn kernels into pan. Cover and simmer until salmon is just cooked through, about 3 minutes. Stir in pureed corn and cook 1 minute more.

PER SERVING (1½ cups): 361 Cal, 8 g Total Fat, 2 g Sat Fat, 0 g Trans Fat, 49 mg Chol, 734 mg Sod, 20 g Carb, 5 g Sugar, 5 g Fib, 29 g Prot, 84 mg Calc.

FYI

Pureeing corn kernels with a little fat-free half-and-half is a smart way to add sweetness and silkiness to this soup without excess fat. If you're not a fan of lima beans, use 1⅓ cups frozen peas instead.

SPICY TORTELLINI AND ROAST TOMATO SOUP

SERVES 4

- ▲ 2 cups frozen sliced bell pepper and onion blend
- 2 garlic cloves, minced
- ▲ 2 cups reduced-sodium chicken broth
- ▲ 1 (15-ounce) can no-salt-added fire-roasted diced tomatoes
- 1 cup water
- ⅛ teaspoon salt
- 1½ cups refrigerated whole wheat three-cheese tortellini (6 ounces)
- 2 tablespoons chopped fresh basil or cilantro
- ▲ 1 tablespoon sliced pickled jalapeño (no sugar added), minced

1 Combine bell pepper blend, garlic, broth, tomatoes, water, and salt in large saucepan. Bring to boil over high heat. Reduce heat; cover and simmer 5 minutes.

2 Stir in tortellini. Return to boil; reduce heat and simmer until tortellini are tender, about 8 minutes. Stir in basil and jalapeño.

PER SERVING (1¼ cups): 191 Cal, 5 g Total Fat, 2 g Sat Fat, 0 g Trans Fat, 24 mg Chol, 331 mg Sod, 26 g Carb, 7 g Sugar, 4 g Fib, 10 g Prot, 84 mg Calc.

5 PointsPlus value

Deli-Delicious Lunches

SMOKED CHICKEN WALDORF SALAD

SERVES 4 • READY IN 20 MIN OR LESS

2 tablespoons fat-free mayonnaise

▲ 1 tablespoon fat-free plain yogurt

2 tablespoons red wine vinegar

2 teaspoons Dijon mustard

¼ teaspoon black pepper

½ pound smoked chicken breast, in one piece

▲ 1 Granny Smith apple, cored and thinly sliced

▲ 1 cup red grapes, halved

▲ 1 celery stalk, thinly sliced

▲ ¼ small red onion, chopped

¼ cup walnut halves, chopped

▲ 4 cups baby salad greens

Whisk together mayonnaise, yogurt, vinegar, mustard, and pepper in large bowl. Cut chicken into thin strips. Add chicken, apple, grapes, celery, onion, and walnuts to dressing and toss to combine. Serve over salad greens.

PER SERVING (1½ cups chicken salad and 1 cup greens): 180 Cal, 6 g Total Fat, 1 g Sat Fat, 0 g Trans Fat, 31 mg Chol, 663 mg Sod, 24 g Carb, 16 g Sugar, 4 g Fib, 12 g Prot, 33 mg Calc.

FYI

Serve this salad with a side of crunchy whole grain crackers. A ½-ounce serving of whole wheat crackers has a *PointsPlus* value of *2.*

TURKEY NACHO SALAD

SERVES 4 • READY IN 20 MIN OR LESS

▲ 4 cups packaged coleslaw mix

1 cup lightly packed fresh cilantro leaves

2 tablespoons rice vinegar

▲ 1 tablespoon sliced pickled jalapeño (no sugar added), chopped

1 teaspoon chili powder

▲ ½ pound lower-sodium fat-free roast turkey breast, in 1 piece

▲ 1 cup canned no-salt-added kidney beans, rinsed and drained

1 ounce (about 12) baked tortilla chips, crumbled

▲ ¾ cup fat-free salsa

▲ ¼ cup fat-free sour cream

▲ 2 scallions, thinly sliced

Toss coleslaw mix, cilantro, vinegar, jalapeño, and chili powder together in large bowl. Divide among 4 plates. Dice turkey and evenly divide among plates. Top evenly with beans, tortilla chips, salsa, and sour cream. Sprinkle with scallions.

PER SERVING (1 salad): 192 Cal, 3 g Total Fat, 1 g Sat Fat, 0 g Trans Fat, 32 mg Chol, 799 mg Sod, 28 g Carb, 4 g Sugar, 7 g Fib, 16 g Prot, 96 mg Calc.

5 PointsPlus© value™

Deli-Delicious Lunches

OURS vs. THEIRS

Planning ahead really pays off when it comes to lunch. Putting together a quick salad or sandwich yourself and either eating it at home or brown-bagging it to school or to the office will save money and give you more delicious eating options. Here's how some of our simple recipes for popular lunch options compare to common diner and restaurant versions.

YOUR CHOICE	OURS	THEIRS	WITH YOUR SAVINGS TRY
CHICKEN SANDWICH	One of our Santa Fe Chicken Paninis, p. 37: *7 PointsPlus* value	Grilled fast-food chicken sandwich (6 ¾ ounces): *10 PointsPlus* value	1 cup tomato soup: *3 PointsPlus* value
TUNA SALAD	A serving of our Spicy Tuna Salad Rolls, p. 41: *8 PointsPlus* value	6¼-ounce diner-style tuna salad sandwich: *11 PointsPlus* value	½-cup scoop of fat-free frozen yogurt: *3 PointsPlus* value
CHEESEBURGER	One of our Green Chile and Cheddar Turkey Burgers, p. 43: *7 PointsPlus* value	Small fast-food cheeseburger on a bun with condiments and vegetables: *10 PointsPlus* value	⅓ cup store-bought coleslaw: *3 PointsPlus* value
WALDORF SALAD	A serving of our Smoked Chicken Waldorf Salad, p. 50: *5 PointsPlus* value	1 cup of regular Waldorf salad: *11 PointsPlus* value	¼ cup reduced-fat honey roasted peanuts and 1⅓ cups fat-free cottage cheese: *6 PointsPlus* value total
NACHOS	A serving of our Turkey Nacho Salad, p. 51: *5 PointsPlus* value	4-ounce fast-food serving of nachos with cheese: *9 PointsPlus* value	1 ounce regular granola bar: *4 PointsPlus* value

SALMON PASTA SALAD WITH SUGAR SNAPS AND DILL

SERVES 4

- ▲ 4 ounces whole wheat rotini pasta
- ▲ 1 cup sugar snap peas, strings removed
- ▲ ¼ cup plain fat-free Greek yogurt
- 3 tablespoons fat-free mayonnaise
- 2 tablespoons chopped fresh dill
- 1 teaspoon grated lemon zest
- 2 tablespoons lemon juice
- ¼ teaspoon black pepper
- ▲ 1 cup grape tomatoes, halved
- ▲ 2 scallions, thinly sliced
- ▲ 1 (14¾-ounce) can water-packed wild salmon, drained, skin and large bones discarded

1 Cook pasta according to package directions, omitting salt and adding sugar snap peas during last minute of cooking. Drain in colander. Cool under cold running water; drain again.

2 Whisk together yogurt, mayonnaise, dill, lemon zest and juice, and pepper in large bowl. Add pasta and sugar snaps, tomatoes, and scallions; toss to combine. Break salmon into large chunks and gently stir into pasta mixture.

PER SERVING (generous 1½ cups): 306 Cal, 8 g Total Fat, 1 g Sat Fat, 0 g Trans Fat, 73 mg Chol, 519 mg Sod, 24 g Carb, 5 g Sugar, 5 g Fib, 35 g Prot, 72 mg Calc.

7 PointsPlus© value

FYI

If you want to make the salad ahead, refrigerate the yogurt dressing and salad separately up to 2 days ahead, and toss together just before serving. This will keep the vegetables crisp and the flavors bright.

TUNA AND NEW POTATO SALAD
WITH BASIL DRESSING

TUNA AND NEW POTATO SALAD WITH BASIL DRESSING

SERVES 4

- ▲ ¾ pound small red potatoes
- ¼ cup chopped fresh basil
- 2 tablespoons red wine vinegar
- 1 tablespoon lemon juice
- 2½ teaspoons olive oil
- 4 teaspoons Dijon mustard
- ¼ teaspoon salt
- ¼ teaspoon black pepper
- ▲ 4 small tomatoes, cut into wedges
- ▲ ½ cup roasted red bell pepper (not oil-packed), cut into chunks
- ▲ 1 (12-ounce) can no-salt-added water-packed solid white tuna, drained and broken into chunks
- ▲ 4 cups sliced or torn romaine lettuce leaves

❶ Prick potatoes with tip of paring knife. Place in microwavable bowl; cover bowl with plastic and vent one corner. Microwave on High until potatoes are tender, about 5 minutes. Set aside to cool slightly, and cut into 1-inch pieces.

❷ Whisk together basil, vinegar, lemon juice, oil, mustard, salt, and pepper in large bowl. Add potatoes, tomatoes, and roasted bell pepper to bowl with dressing; toss to coat. Gently stir in tuna. Spoon tuna mixture over lettuce and serve.

PER SERVING (1¼ cups tuna mixture and 1 cup lettuce): 257 Cal, 6 g Total Fat, 1 g Sat Fat, 0 g Trans Fat, 36 mg Chol, 433 mg Sod, 26 g Carb, 5 g Sugar, 5 g Fib, 24 g Prot, 64 mg Calc.

Deli-Delicious Lunches

FYI

If you like, sprinkle the salad with a tablespoon of capers. Serve it with a small bunch of crisp grapes or a few wedges of ripe honeydew.

CHAPTER 3

Everything Italian

Appetizers

ESCAROLE SOUP WITH BARLEY AND CANNELLINI

MUSHROOMS STUFFED WITH SAUSAGE AND BROCCOLI RABE

Main Courses

SPICY STEAK PIZZAIOLA

ROAST PORK TONNATO

ROSEMARY CHICKEN WITH FRESH TOMATO AND BALSAMIC SAUCE

CHICKEN MILANESE WITH SAVORY WATERCRESS

SPAGHETTI WITH CHICKEN, ARUGULA, AND BREAD CRUMBS

FETTUCCINE MARSALA WITH CHICKEN AND MUSHROOMS

TURKEY SALTIMBOCCA WITH LEMON AND SAGE

COD CIOPPINO

LINGUINE PESTO WITH SHRIMP AND ASPARAGUS

MUSSELS FRA DIAVOLO WITH FRESH HERBS

GRILLED CALAMARI AND OZRO SALAD

THREE-CHEESE PIZZA WITH GARLICKY SPINACH AND BACON

TORTELLONI WITH BUTTERNUT SQUASH AND KALE

QUINOA AND VEGETABLE RISOTTO

Italian Pantry Partners

KEEP THESE STAPLES ON HAND TO QUICKLY GET HEALTHFUL MEALS ON THE TABLE.

Anchovy Paste Anchovies add robust flavor to sauces, salads, and dressings. Convenient squeezable tubes of paste will keep refrigerated up to 1 year. One-half teaspoon of paste is equivalent to about two anchovy fillets.

Balsamic Vinegar This classic Italian vinegar is dark and thick, with a sweet, concentrated flavor that makes it equally popular for vinaigrettes and as an addition to sauces. Buy a good quality aged balsamic and you can enjoy it drizzled over everything from grilled vegetables to strawberries.

Canned Beans ▲ Cannellini, chickpea, and many other bean varieties are popular in Italian soups, stews, pastas, and salads. No-salt-added canned beans are now readily available and are a good way to reduce the sodium in bean recipes.

Canned Tomatoes ▲ The best and quickest way to bring rich tomato flavor to your dishes year-round is to use canned tomatoes. A great choice is imported Italian San Marzano tomatoes, world-famous for their deep flavor and firm texture even when canned. If you're trying to control your sodium intake, look for cans labeled "no salt added."

Capers These tangy little buds are great for adding zing to sauces and salads. Rinse them under cold water to remove excess salt.

Dried Pastas Most of our recipes call for whole wheat pastas since they are slightly higher in fiber and protein than standard pastas. Brands vary widely in texture so experiment to find one you and your family really like.

Olive Oil Italian extra-virgin olive oils are known for their fruity rich flavor and low acidity. All our recipes will turn out wonderfully with a moderately priced blended oil, although you might want to invest in a really good oil made from olives of a single estate to use in uncooked dishes like vinaigrettes.

Olives Olives bring a burst of flavor to just about any dish. Choose imported brine-cured olives in jars or in bulk from an olive bar over the bland, canned, mealy ones from California.

Parmesan Cheese Parmesan is ubiquitous in Italian cooking, bringing salty tang and a hint of richness to everything from salads to soups to pastas. Aged imported Parmesan is the gold standard, although a number of domestic varieties, including reduced-fat Parmesan, are also available and work well in most dishes.

Prebaked Pizza Crusts Nothing beats these crusts for making a quick, easy custom pie. A number of good-quality crusts are now available in both white and extra-healthful whole grain.

ESCAROLE SOUP WITH BARLEY AND CANNELLINI

SERVES 6 AS AN APPETIZER

2   teaspoons olive oil

▲ 2   carrots, diced

▲ 1   large leek, cleaned and thinly sliced, white and light green parts only

3   garlic cloves, minced

▲ 1   bunch escarole, cleaned and coarsely chopped

▲ 5   cups reduced-sodium chicken broth

▲ 2   (15½-ounce) cans no-salt-added cannellini (white kidney) beans, rinsed and drained

▲ ¾   cup quick-cooking barley

1   cup water

6   teaspoons shredded or shaved Parmesan cheese

❶ Heat oil in Dutch oven over medium-high heat. Add carrots, leek, and garlic; cook, stirring occasionally, until vegetables soften, about 5 minutes.

❷ Add escarole, broth, beans, barley, and water; bring to boil. Reduce heat and simmer, partially covered, until barley is tender, about 10 minutes. Serve sprinkled with Parmesan.

PER SERVING (1½ cups soup and 1 teaspoon cheese): 287 Cal, 5 g Total Fat, 1 g Sat Fat, 0 g Trans Fat, 1 mg Chol, 169 mg Sod, 48 g Carb, 3 g Sugar, 13 g Fib, 15 g Prot, 140 mg Calc.

7 PointsPlus® value

ESCAROLE SOUP WITH
BARLEY AND CANNELLINI

OURS vs. THEIRS

Everyone loves Italian! Try some of our delicious, healthful recipes at home and you can enjoy many of your favorite dishes without exceeding your daily *PointsPlus* Target. Here's how some of the recipes in this chapter match up against versions you might find at your local trattoria.

YOUR CHOICE	OURS	THEIRS	WITH YOUR SAVINGS TRY
TONNATO	A serving of our Roast Pork Tonnato, p. 66: *5 PointsPlus* value	Restaurant-style vitello tonnato made with 2 slices veal and ½ cup sauce: *16 PointsPlus* value	1 cup minestrone soup and 2 amaretti cookies: *11 PointsPlus* value total
CHICKEN MARSALA	A serving of our Fettuccine Marsala with Chicken and Mushrooms, p. 71: *7 PointsPlus* value	A 4-ounce serving of restaurant-style chicken marsala with sauce: *14 PointsPlus* value	6 baked clams: *7 PointsPlus* value
CIOPPINO	A serving of our Cod Cioppino, p. 73: *4 PointsPlus* value	2 cups restaurant-style cioppino: *13 PointsPlus* value	1 (3-ounce) piece store-bought focaccia bread and 3 small (½-ounce) chocolate biscotti: *9 PointsPlus* value total
PIZZA	A serving of our Three-Cheese Pizza with Garlicky Spinach and Bacon, p. 78: *7 PointsPlus* value	1 large slice thin-crust pizza with 1 meat topping from a pizzeria: *8 PointsPlus* value	Green salad dressed with 1 tablespoon Italian vinaigrette: *1 PointsPlus* value total
RISOTTO	A serving of our Quinoa and Vegetable Risotto, p. 81: *5 PointsPlus* value	1-cup serving of restaurant-style risotto: *11 PointsPlus* value	2 servings (2) of our Mushrooms Stuffed with Sausage and Broccoli Rabe, p. 63: *6 PointsPlus* value

MUSHROOMS STUFFED WITH SAUSAGE AND BROCCOLI RABE

SERVES 6 AS AN APPETIZER

- ▲ **1** bunch broccoli rabe, trimmed and coarsely chopped
- **2** teaspoons olive oil
- **⅓** pound sweet Italian turkey sausage, casings removed
- **2** garlic cloves, minced
- **¼** teaspoon red pepper flakes, or to taste
- ▲ **¼** cup reduced-sodium chicken broth
- **2** tablespoons dried whole wheat bread crumbs

Pinch salt

- **3** tablespoons grated Parmesan cheese
- ▲ **6** (4-inch) portobello mushroom caps

1 Bring medium pot of water to boil. Add broccoli rabe, return to boil, and cook until tender, about 5 minutes. Drain. Cool under cold running water; drain again. Squeeze dry and chop finely. Transfer to large bowl.

2 Meanwhile, preheat broiler. Spray small baking pan with nonstick spray.

3 Heat 1 teaspoon oil in small nonstick skillet over medium-high heat. Add sausage, garlic, and pepper flakes and cook, breaking up sausage with spoon, until sausage is browned, about 5 minutes. Add to broccoli rabe in bowl along with broth, bread crumbs, salt, and 2 tablespoons of Parmesan; toss to mix.

4 Place mushrooms caps, rounded side down, on pan. Spoon sausage filling evenly into caps; sprinkle with remaining 1 tablespoon cheese and drizzle with remaining 1 teaspoon oil. Broil 6 inches from heat until filling is hot and topping is browned, about 6 minutes.

PER SERVING (1 stuffed mushroom): 113 Cal, 5 g Total Fat, 1 g Sat Fat, 0 g Trans Fat, 17 mg Chol, 271 mg Sod, 8 g Carb, 3 g Sugar, 1 g Fib, 9 g Prot, 61 mg Calc.

3 PointsPlus® value

Everything Italian

SPICY STEAK PIZZAIOLA

SERVES 4

3 teaspoons olive oil

1 small onion, thinly sliced

4 garlic cloves, minced

¼ teaspoon red pepper flakes, or to taste

1 (15-ounce) can Italian peeled tomatoes

1 teaspoon dried oregano

½ teaspoon salt

3 tablespoons coarsely chopped flat-leaf parsley

1 (1-pound) lean boneless sirloin steak, trimmed

½ small (8-ounce) whole wheat baguette

1 Heat 2 teaspoons of oil in medium saucepan over medium-high heat. Add onion, 3 cloves of garlic, and pepper flakes. Cook, stirring occasionally, until onion softens, about 5 minutes. Add tomatoes, ½ teaspoon oregano, and ¼ teaspoon salt; bring to boil. Reduce heat and simmer, stirring occasionally and breaking up tomatoes, until sauce thickens slightly, about 8 minutes. Stir in parsley.

2 Spray broiler pan with nonstick spray; preheat broiler. Sprinkle steak with remaining ¼ teaspoon salt. Place steak on pan and broil, turning once, until instant-read thermometer inserted into center of steak registers 145°F for medium, about 5 minutes per side. Transfer to cutting board; let stand 5 minutes.

3 Split baguette lengthwise, then cut each piece in half again, making 4 equal pieces. Mix remaining 1 teaspoon oil, remaining garlic clove, and remaining ½ teaspoon oregano in small bowl. Brush mixture on cut sides of bread. Place bread, cut-side up, on broiler rack and broil until lightly browned. Cut steak into 12 slices. Serve with sauce and bread.

PER SERVING (3 slices steak, ½ cup sauce, and 1 piece garlic bread): 274 Cal, 9 g Total Fat, 2 g Sat Fat, 0 g Trans Fat, 42 mg Chol, 721 mg Sod, 22 g Carb, 4 g Sugar, 3 g Fib, 27 g Prot, 48 mg Calc.

7 PointsPlus® value

Everything Italian

ROAST PORK TONNATO

SERVES 4

▲ 1 (1-pound) pork tenderloin, trimmed

1 teaspoon olive oil

1 teaspoon chopped fresh thyme

▲ 1 (5-ounce) can water-packed light tuna, drained and flaked

⅓ cup reduced-fat mayonnaise

Grated zest and juice of 1 lemon

2 tablespoons capers, rinsed and drained

1 tablespoon chopped flat-leaf parsley

2 teaspoons anchovy paste

1 lemon, cut into 8 wedges

❶ Preheat oven to 450°F. Spray small roasting pan with nonstick spray.

❷ Rub pork with oil and sprinkle with thyme. Place pork in roasting pan and roast until instant-read thermometer inserted into center of pork registers 145°F for medium, about 20 minutes. Transfer pork to cutting board and let stand 5 minutes. Cut into 12 slices.

❸ Meanwhile, combine tuna, mayonnaise, lemon zest and juice, capers, parsley, and anchovy paste in medium bowl and stir to combine. Fan pork slices over platter and top with sauce. Serve with lemon wedges.

PER SERVING (3 slices pork with ¼ cup sauce): 215 Cal, 8 g Total Fat, 2 g Sat Fat, 0 g Trans Fat, 90 mg Chol, 661 mg Sod, 4 g Carb, 2 g Sugar, 1 g Fib, 31 g Prot, 14 mg Calc.

FYI

Turn this dish into a delicious main-course salad by serving it over a bed of 6 cups mixed greens and 2 cups coarsely chopped steamed green beans tossed with a little lemon juice.

ROSEMARY CHICKEN WITH FRESH TOMATO AND BALSAMIC SAUCE

SERVES 4

- ▲ 4 (¼-pound) thin-sliced skinless boneless chicken cutlets
- 2 teaspoons chopped fresh rosemary
- ½ teaspoon salt
- 2 teaspoons olive oil
- 2 shallots, thinly sliced
- 2 garlic cloves, minced
- 2 tablespoons balsamic vinegar
- ▲ 2 cups red or yellow cherry tomatoes (or a mix of both), halved
- ▲ ¼ cup reduced-sodium chicken broth
- 2 teaspoons capers, rinsed and drained
- 1 tablespoon grated lemon zest

❶ Sprinkle chicken with ½ teaspoon rosemary and ¼ teaspoon salt. Heat oil in large nonstick skillet over medium-high heat. Add chicken and cook just until browned and cooked through, 2–3 minutes per side. Transfer chicken to platter and keep warm.

❷ Add shallots and garlic to skillet; cook over medium heat, stirring, until softened, about 2 minutes. Add vinegar; cook, stirring with wooden spoon and scraping up any browned bits from bottom of pan, until vinegar is evaporated. Stir in tomatoes, broth, capers, lemon zest, remaining 1½ teaspoons rosemary, and remaining ¼ teaspoon salt. Cook, stirring frequently, until tomatoes are softened, about 3 minutes. Return chicken and any accumulated juices to skillet; heat through.

PER SERVING (1 chicken cutlet with ⅓ cup sauce):
179 Cal, 5 g Total Fat, 1 g Sat Fat, 0 g Trans Fat, 63 mg Chol, 400 mg Sod, 8 g Carb, 4 g Sugar, 1 g Fib, 24 g Prot, 33 mg Calc.

CHICKEN MILANESE WITH SAVORY WATERCRESS

SERVES 4

- ▲ 2 **large egg whites**
- 2 **teaspoons Dijon mustard**
- ½ **cup whole wheat panko (bread crumbs)**
- 2 **tablespoons chopped flat-leaf parsley**

Zest of 1 lemon

- ▲ 4 **(5-ounce) skinless boneless chicken breasts**
- 1 **tablespoon lemon juice**
- 2 **teaspoons olive oil**
- ¼ **teaspoon salt**
- ▲ 1 **bunch watercress, trimmed**
- ▲ ½ **small red onion, thinly sliced**
- ¼ **cup shaved Parmesan cheese**

❶ Place rack in top third of oven. Preheat to 425°F. Spray baking sheet with nonstick spray.

❷ Whisk together egg whites and mustard in shallow bowl. Combine panko, parsley, and zest on wax paper. Dip chicken pieces, one at a time, into egg mixture, then into panko mixture, pressing gently to coat. Place on baking sheet and lightly spray with nonstick spray. Bake 10 minutes. Turn chicken and lightly spray with nonstick spray. Bake until browned and cooked through, about 10 minutes longer.

❸ Whisk together lemon juice, oil, and salt in bowl. Add watercress and onion; toss to coat. Place a chicken breast on each of 4 plates. Top with watercress mixture and Parmesan.

PER SERVING (1 cutlet, 1½ cups salad, and 1 tablespoon cheese): 245 Cal, 7 g Total Fat, 2 g Sat Fat, 0 g Trans Fat, 82 mg Chol, 533 mg Sod, 9 g Carb, 1 g Sugar, 1 g Fib, 35 g Prot, 138 mg Calc.

FYI

To make Parmesan shavings, start with a small wedge of cheese and use a vegetable peeler to shave off thin strips with a firm, downward motion.

CHICKEN MILANESE WITH
SAVORY WATERCRESS

SPAGHETTI WITH CHICKEN, ARUGULA, AND BREAD CRUMBS

SERVES 4

- ▲ **6 ounces whole wheat spaghetti**
- ▲ **½ pound chicken tenders, cut into thin strips**
- **½ teaspoon salt**
- **2 teaspoons olive oil**
- **1 large shallot, thinly sliced**
- **2 garlic cloves, thinly sliced**
- **¼ teaspoon red pepper flakes**
- ▲ **6 cups baby arugula**
- **Zest and juice of 1 lemon**
- **3 tablespoons dried whole wheat bread crumbs**

1 Cook spaghetti according to package directions, omitting salt. Drain, reserving ¼ cup cooking water.

2 Meanwhile, sprinkle chicken with salt. Heat oil in large nonstick skillet over medium-high heat. Add chicken and cook, turning occasionally, until chicken is browned and cooked through, 3–4 minutes. Add shallot, garlic, and pepper flakes and cook, stirring constantly, 1 minute.

3 Stir in spaghetti, arugula, lemon zest and juice, and reserved pasta water. Cook, stirring, just until arugula begins to wilt, about 1 minute. Add bread crumbs and toss to coat.

PER SERVING (1¼ cups): 270 Cal, 5 g Total Fat, 1 g Sat Fat, 0 g Trans Fat, 31 mg Chol, 392 mg Sod, 39 g Carb, 4 g Sugar, 7 g Fib, 20 g Prot, 95 mg Calc.

7 PointsPlus© value

FYI

Make a quick and easy tricolor salad to serve with this pasta: Toss together 6 cups chopped escarole, 1 small head sliced radicchio, 1 head sliced Belgian endive, a splash of red wine vinegar, and salt and black pepper to taste.

FETTUCCINE MARSALA WITH CHICKEN AND MUSHROOMS

SERVES 6

- 6   ounces whole wheat fettuccine
- 1   pound skinless boneless chicken thighs, cut into 2-inch pieces
- ½   teaspoon salt
- 2   teaspoons olive oil
- ¾   pound cremini mushrooms, halved
- 1   teaspoon chopped fresh rosemary
- 2   garlic cloves, minced
- 1   tablespoon all-purpose flour
- 1   cup thawed frozen pearl onions
- ½   cup dry Marsala wine
- ⅓   cup reduced-sodium chicken broth
- ¼   teaspoon black pepper

① Cook fettuccine according to package directions, omitting salt. Drain and keep warm.

② Sprinkle chicken with ¼ teaspoon salt. Heat 1 teaspoon oil in large nonstick skillet over medium-high heat. Add chicken and cook, turning occasionally, until browned and cooked through, 3–4 minutes. Transfer to plate.

③ Add mushrooms, rosemary, garlic, and remaining 1 teaspoon oil to skillet. Cook over medium-high heat, stirring occasionally, until mushrooms are soft, about 3 minutes. Stir in flour and cook 1 minute longer.

④ Add pearl onions, wine, broth, pepper, and remaining ¼ teaspoon salt; bring to boil. Reduce heat and simmer, stirring occasionally, until sauce thickens slightly, 3–4 minutes. Return chicken and any accumulated juices to skillet. Add fettuccine; toss coat with sauce and cook until heated through, 1–2 minutes.

PER SERVING (generous 1 cup): 289 Cal, 9 g Total Fat, 2 g Sat Fat, 0 g Trans Fat, 50 mg Chol, 259 mg Sod, 26 g Carb, 4 g Sugar, 5 g Fib, 20 g Prot, 36 mg Calc.

7 PointsPlus value

TURKEY SALTIMBOCCA WITH LEMON AND SAGE

SERVES 4

▲ 4 (¼-pound) skinless turkey cutlets

2 very thin slices prosciutto (about 1 ounce), each cut lengthwise in half

4 (½-ounce) slices light Jarlsberg cheese

▲ ½ cup thawed frozen chopped spinach, squeezed dry

½ teaspoon salt

2 teaspoons olive oil

1 shallot, thinly sliced

1 teaspoon all-purpose flour

▲ ¾ cup reduced-sodium chicken broth

Zest and juice of 1 lemon

2 teaspoons chopped fresh sage

❶ Place 1 cutlet between 2 sheets of wax paper; gently pound with wooden mallet or rolling pin until meat is ¼ inch thick. Top with 1 piece prosciutto, 1 slice Jarlsberg, and 2 table-spoons spinach. Roll up turkey to enclose filling and secure with wooden toothpick. Repeat with remaining turkey, prosciutto, cheese, and spinach. Sprinkle rolls with ¼ teaspoon salt.

❷ Heat 1 teaspoon oil in large nonstick skillet over medium-high heat. Add turkey rolls and cook, turning frequently, until lightly browned, about 5 minutes. Transfer rolls to plate.

❸ Heat remaining 1 teaspoon oil in same skillet over medium-high heat. Add shallot and cook, stirring, until softened, 1–2 minutes. Sprinkle shallot with flour; cook, stirring, 1 minute. Whisk in broth, lemon zest and juice, sage, and remaining ¼ teaspoon salt; simmer, stirring, until sauce thickens slightly. Return turkey rolls to skillet. Reduce heat and simmer, uncovered, until rolls are heated through, 2–3 minutes. Remove toothpicks; serve rolls with sauce.

PER SERVING (1 roll and 3 tablespoons sauce):
214 Cal, 6 g Total Fat, 2 g Sat Fat, 0 g Trans Fat, 57 mg Chol, 712 mg Sod, 5 g Carb, 1 g Sugar, 1 g Fib, 36 g Prot, 160 mg Calc.

5 PointsPlus value

COD CIOPPINO

SERVES 4

2 teaspoons olive oil

▲ 1 onion, chopped

▲ 1 green bell pepper, diced

4 garlic cloves, chopped

▲ 1 yellow squash, diced

▲ 1 cup reduced-sodium chicken broth

▲ 1 cup canned diced no-salt-added tomatoes

¼ cup dry red wine

½ teaspoon salt

Pinch cayenne

▲ 1 pound cod, cut into 1-inch pieces

2 tablespoons chopped flat-leaf parsley

❶ Heat oil in large nonstick saucepan over medium-high heat. Add onion, bell pepper, and garlic and cook, stirring occasionally, until softened, about 6 minutes. Add squash, broth, tomatoes, wine, salt, and cayenne; bring to boil. Reduce heat, cover, and simmer 10 minutes.

❷ Add cod and cook until fish is just opaque in center, about 5 minutes. Stir in parsley.

PER SERVING (1¼ cups): 169 Cal, 4 g Total Fat, 1 g Sat Fat, 0 g Trans Fat, 43 mg Chol, 383 mg Sod, 11 g Carb, 6 g Sugar, 2 g Fib, 21 g Prot, 53 mg Calc.

FYI

Good substitutes for cod in this soup include mahimahi, halibut, or bay scallops.

LINGUINE PESTO WITH
SHRIMP AND ASPARAGUS

LINGUINE PESTO WITH SHRIMP AND ASPARAGUS

SERVES 4

▲ 6 ounces whole wheat linguine

▲ 1 (1-pound) bunch asparagus, trimmed and cut into 2-inch pieces

2 teaspoons olive oil

▲ ¾ pound peeled, deveined medium shrimp

3 garlic cloves, minced

¼ teaspoon red pepper flakes

▲ 1 (14-ounce) can Italian peeled tomatoes

¼ teaspoon salt

2 tablespoons prepared pesto

Grated zest of 1 lemon

6 pitted black olives (not cured in oil), chopped

❶ Cook linguine according to package directions, omitting salt, and adding asparagus during last 1 minute of cooking. Drain and keep warm.

❷ Meanwhile, heat 1 teaspoon oil in large nonstick skillet over medium-high heat. Add shrimp, garlic, and pepper flakes; cook, stirring frequently, just until shrimp turn pink, about 2 minutes. Transfer to plate.

❸ Heat remaining 1 teaspoon oil in same skillet over medium-high heat. Add tomatoes and salt and cook, stirring occasionally and breaking up tomatoes with side of spoon, just until sauce begins to thicken, about 5 minutes. Return shrimp to the skillet. Add linguine, asparagus, pesto, and lemon zest; cook, tossing, until heated through. Remove from heat; sprinkle with olives.

PER SERVING (1⅓ cups): 333 Cal, 10 g Total Fat, 2 g Sat Fat, 0 g Trans Fat, 129 mg Chol, 641 mg Sod, 38 g Carb, 7 g Sugar, 10 g Fib, 25 g Prot, 124 mg Calc.

MUSSELS FRA DIAVOLO WITH FRESH HERBS

SERVES 4 • READY IN 20 MIN OR LESS

2 teaspoons olive oil

4 garlic cloves, finely chopped

▲ 1 (28-ounce) can Italian peeled tomatoes

½ cup dry white wine

1 teaspoon chopped fresh rosemary

½ teaspoon red pepper flakes, or to taste

¼ teaspoon salt

▲ 2½ pounds mussels, scrubbed and debearded

¼ cup chopped fresh basil

2 teaspoons chopped fresh thyme

❶ Heat oil in Dutch oven over medium-high heat. Add garlic and cook, stirring constantly, 1 minute. Add tomatoes, wine, rosemary, pepper flakes, and salt; bring to boil. Reduce heat and simmer, uncovered, stirring occasionally and breaking up tomatoes with side of spoon, until sauce begins to thicken, 8–10 minutes.

❷ Increase heat to medium-high; add mussels. Cover and cook until mussels open, about 4 minutes. Discard any mussels that do not open. With slotted spoon, divide mussels evenly among 4 serving bowls. Stir basil and thyme into sauce in Dutch oven. Ladle sauce evenly over mussels.

PER SERVING (about 16 mussels with ¾ cup sauce):
145 Cal, 4 g Total Fat, 1 g Sat Fat, 0 g Trans Fat, 17 mg Chol, 746 mg Sod, 12 g Carb, 5 g Sugar, 2 g Fib, 9 g Prot, 61 mg Calc.

FYI

Serve these tangy, spicy mussels with toast points for dipping. Two slices of reduced-calorie whole-grain or white bread per serving will increase the *PointsPlus* value by **3.**

GRILLED CALAMARI AND ORZO SALAD

SERVES 4 • READY IN 20 MIN OR LESS

▲ ½ cup whole wheat orzo

▲ 1 pound fresh or thawed frozen
      cleaned calamari

  2 teaspoons olive oil

  ½ teaspoon salt

  ½ teaspoon black pepper

▲ 1 pint grape tomatoes, halved

▲ 1 (7-ounce) jar roasted red bell peppers
      (not oil-packed), thinly sliced

▲ ¼ cup sliced scallions

  1 tablespoon capers, rinsed and drained

  Zest and juice of ½ lemon

  ¼ cup chopped fresh parsley

▲ 6 cups baby arugula

❶ Cook orzo according to package directions, omitting salt. Drain in colander and rinse under cold running water. Drain again and put into large bowl.

❷ Meanwhile, spray nonstick ridged grill pan with nonstick spray; set over medium-high heat. Toss calamari with 1 teaspoon oil, ¼ teaspoon salt, and ¼ teaspoon black pepper. Place in pan and grill, turning occasionally, until cooked through, about 6 minutes. Transfer to cutting board.

❸ Cut calamari bodies into ½-inch-thick rings and tentacles into small sections; add to bowl with orzo. Add tomatoes, roasted bell peppers, scallions, capers, lemon zest and juice, parsley, remaining 1 teaspoon olive oil, remaining ¼ teaspoon salt, and remaining ¼ teaspoon black pepper and toss to combine.

❹ Divide arugula among 4 plates and top with calamari salad.

PER SERVING (1½ cups calamari salad and 1½ cups arugula): 243 Cal, 5 g Total Fat, 1 g Sat Fat, 0 g Trans Fat, 264 mg Chol, 600 mg Sod, 26 g Carb, 4 g Sugar, 5 g Fib, 24 g Prot, 111 mg Calc.

6 PointsPlus© value™

Everything Italian

THREE-CHEESE PIZZA WITH GARLICKY SPINACH AND BACON

SERVES 4 • READY IN 20 MIN OR LESS

3 slices turkey bacon, chopped

2 garlic cloves, thinly sliced

▲ **1** (5-ounce) package baby spinach leaves

1 (10-ounce) prebaked whole wheat thin pizza crust

▲ **⅔** cup fat-free ricotta cheese

▲ **½** cup fat-free shredded mozzarella cheese

2 tablespoons grated Parmesan cheese

❶ Preheat oven to 450°F. Spray large baking sheet with nonstick spray.

❷ Spray large nonstick skillet with nonstick spray and set over medium-high heat. Add bacon and cook, stirring occasionally, until browned, about 5 minutes. Transfer bacon to plate lined with paper towels.

❸ Add garlic to skillet; cook over medium heat, stirring constantly, until golden, about 1 minute. Add spinach to skillet a few handfuls at a time, stirring constantly and adding more spinach as it will fit. Continue cooking until spinach is wilted, about 2 minutes more. Stir in reserved bacon.

❹ Place crust on baking sheet. Spread ricotta evenly over crust. Top evenly with spinach mixture. Sprinkle with mozzarella and Parmesan. Bake until cheese is bubbling, about 8 minutes. Cut into 8 pieces.

PER SERVING (2 pieces pizza): 283 Cal, 6 g Total Fat, 1 g Sat Fat, 0 g Trans Fat, 18 mg Chol, 787 mg Sod, 38 g Carb, 1 g Sugar, 5 g Fib, 20 g Prot, 340 mg Calc.

THREE-CHEESE PIZZA
WITH GARLICKY SPINACH
AND BACON

TORTELLONI WITH BUTTERNUT SQUASH AND KALE

SERVES 4

1   (9-ounce) package three-cheese tortelloni

2   teaspoons olive oil

3   garlic cloves, minced

▲ 1   (20-ounce) package cut and peeled butternut squash, cut into ¾-inch chunks

▲ 1   bunch kale, stems removed and discarded, leaves coarsely chopped

▲ 2   cups reduced-sodium vegetable broth

▲ ¼   cup fat-free half-and-half

Grated zest of 1 orange

Pinch grated nutmeg

1   tablespoon toasted chopped walnuts

❶ Cook tortelloni according to package directions. Drain and keep warm.

❷ Meanwhile, heat oil in large nonstick skillet over medium-high heat. Add garlic and cook, stirring, until softened, about 1 minute. Add squash, kale, and broth; bring to boil. Reduce heat and simmer, covered, until vegetables are tender, about 10 minutes.

❸ Add tortelloni, half-and-half, orange zest, and nutmeg to squash mixture, gently tossing to coat. Sprinkle with walnuts.

PER SERVING (1¼ cups): 342 Cal, 8 g Total Fat, 3 g Sat Fat, 0 g Trans Fat, 24 mg Chol, 402 mg Sod, 57 g Carb, 8 g Sugar, 7 g Fib, 13 g Prot, 278 mg Calc.

9 PointsPlus® value

FYI

Tortelloni are stuffed, rolled pasta that are a bit larger than tortellini. Look for them in the refrigerated or frozen section of your supermarket, or substitute three-cheese tortellini for no change in *PointsPlus* value.

QUINOA AND VEGETABLE RISOTTO

SERVES 4

2   teaspoons olive oil

▲ 1   medium Vidalia onion, chopped

▲ 1   small eggplant (about 10 ounces),
      peeled and cut into ½-inch cubes

▲ 1   zucchini, diced

▲ 2   plum tomatoes, chopped

2   garlic cloves, minced

Pinch salt

▲ ¾   cup quinoa

▲ 1¾ cups vegetable broth

2   tablespoons chopped fresh basil

▲ 2   tablespoons grated fat-free
      Parmesan cheese

❶ Heat oil in large nonstick saucepan over medium-high heat. Add onion, eggplant, zucchini, tomatoes, garlic, and salt. Cook, stirring occasionally, until vegetables are softened, about 5 minutes.

❷ Meanwhile, place quinoa in a fine-mesh strainer and rinse under cold water, tossing occasionally, for 30 seconds.

❸ Add broth and quinoa to saucepan; bring to boil. Reduce heat and simmer, covered, until quinoa is tender and most of the liquid has been absorbed, about 15 minutes. Remove from heat. Stir in basil and sprinkle with Parmesan.

PER SERVING (generous 1 cup): 202 Cal, 5 g Total Fat, 1 g Sat Fat, 0 g Trans Fat, 1 mg Chol, 152 mg Sod, 33 g Carb, 5 g Sugar, 6 g Fib, 8 g Prot, 82 mg Calc.

5
PointsPlus⊕
value

CHAPTER 4

Mexican
and More

Appetizers

CEVICHE-STYLE SHRIMP SALAD WITH MANGO AND AVOCADO

ENLIGHTENED GUACAMOLE WITH JICAMA DIPPING STICKS

Main Courses

SKIRT STEAK FAJITAS WITH SWEET ONION

CARNE ASADA TACOS

PORK AND GREEN CHILE POSOLE STEW

TOSTADOS WITH PORK AND CHIPOTLE CREAM

TOMATILLO ENCHILADAS WITH GRILLED CHICKEN

CHICKEN MOLE WITH YELLOW RICE

CHICKEN CHALUPAS WITH GOAT CHEESE

TAMALE POT PIES WITH TURKEY AND PEPPER JACK

TURKEY PICADILLO WITH CILANTRO RICE

BAHIAN FISH STEW

FISH TACOS WITH TANGY CILANTRO SLAW

BAKED PLANTAINS WITH RICE AND BEANS

MUSHROOM AND GOAT CHEESE QUESADILLAS

Mexican Pantry Partners

KEEP THESE STAPLES ON HAND TO QUICKLY GET
HEALTHFUL MEALS ON THE TABLE.

Canned Beans ▲ Pinto beans, kidney beans, and black beans are favorites in Mexican and Latin cooking. No-salt-added canned beans are now readily available and are a good way to reduce the sodium in bean recipes.

Canned Fat-Free Refried Beans ▲ These tasty mashed beans are excellent for turning something as simple as a tortilla and some veggies into a meal. Or serve them as a side dish with rice dishes or veggie-based entrées.

Canned Green Chiles ▲ There are several varieties of canned green chiles on the market. Most are the very mild Anaheim chiles, although spicier varieties are also available.

Chili Powder This versatile seasoning is made from ground dried chiles plus a number of other flavorings that might include cumin, garlic, or oregano. Most brands are quite mild, although there are some fiery exceptions.

Chipotles en Adobo Chipotles are dried, smoked jalapeño peppers. They're commonly available canned in a rich, lightly sweet tomato sauce. A teaspoon or two of chopped chipotle will bring deep smoky flavor and fiery spice to your dishes.

Cilantro Zesty, extremely aromatic cilantro (a.k.a. coriander) is the ubiquitous fresh herb of Mexican cooking. To keep your cilantro fresh up to a week or more, place the stems in a glass with water as you would a bouquet of flowers. Cover the leaves with a damp paper towel or plastic bag and refrigerate.

Jalapeño Peppers ▲ These are the most popular fresh chiles in Mexican cooking. The good news is that you'll find them in almost any grocery store; the bad news is that they range in heat from mild to very hot, and you'll never know how spicy one is until you taste it. As with all chiles, the heat is concentrated in the seeds and the veins of the jalapeño, so always remove these for a milder taste experience.

Salsa ▲ Having a jar of your favorite fat-free salsa on hand is an easy way to get big flavor into your dishes quickly. We also love pico de gallo for the same reason; look for it in the refrigerated section of your supermarket.

Whole Wheat Flour Tortillas These are a great way to work more whole grains into your diet. Small and medium tortillas are excellent for most taco or enchilada dishes; large (10-inch) ones are popular for burritos and wraps.

CEVICHE-STYLE SHRIMP SALAD
WITH MANGO AND AVOCADO

CEVICHE-STYLE SHRIMP SALAD WITH MANGO AND AVOCADO

SERVES 6 AS AN APPETIZER

¼   cup orange juice

2   tablespoons lemon juice

2   tablespoons lime juice

2   teaspoons olive oil

▲ 1   jalapeño pepper, seeded and minced

1   garlic clove, minced

Pinch salt

▲ ½   pound peeled cooked medium shrimp, chopped

▲ 1   mango, peeled and diced

▲ 1   large plum tomato, diced

▲ ½   small red onion, diced

½   ripe avocado, diced

2   tablespoons chopped fresh cilantro

▲ 2   heads red Belgian endive, separated into leaves

Whisk together orange juice, lemon juice, lime juice, oil, jalapeño, garlic, and salt in large bowl. Add shrimp, mango, tomato, onion, avocado, and cilantro; toss to coat. Chill at least 10 minutes or up to 2 hours. Serve with endive.

PER SERVING (½ cup shrimp mixture and 2–3 endive leaves): 100 Cal, 4 g Total Fat, 1 g Sat Fat, 0 g Trans Fat, 56 mg Chol, 93 mg Sod, 11 g Carb, 6 g Sugar, 2 g Fib, 7 g Prot, 30 mg Calc.

FYI

A traditional ceviche dish relies on an acidic marinade to "cook" raw seafood. We made this super-quick version by starting with cooked and peeled shrimp. A brief marinating helps to meld the flavors in this dish, so, if you have time, make it up to two hours before serving and refrigerate.

ENLIGHTENED GUACAMOLE WITH JICAMA DIPPING STICKS

SERVES 6 AS AN APPETIZER • READY IN 20 MIN OR LESS

1   ripe avocado, peeled and pitted

▲ 1   cup frozen shelled edamame, thawed

3   tablespoons lime juice

1   garlic clove, chopped

¼   cup lightly packed fresh cilantro leaves

¼   cup cold water

1   teaspoon ground cumin

½   teaspoon salt

▲ 1   medium (1½-pound) jicama, peeled, sliced, and cut into ½-inch-wide sticks

¼   teaspoon chili powder

1 Puree avocado, edamame, lime juice, and garlic in food processor. Add cilantro, water, cumin, and ¼ teaspoon salt and pulse until combined.

2 Sprinkle jicama sticks with chili powder and remaining ¼ teaspoon salt; serve with dip.

PER SERVING (generous ¼ cup dip and about 10 jicama sticks): 121 Cal, 6 g Total Fat, 1 g Sat Fat, 0 g Trans Fat, 0 mg Chol, 204 mg Sod, 15 g Carb, 3 g Sugar, 9 g Fib, 4 g Prot, 36 mg Calc.

3 PointsPlus® value

SKIRT STEAK FAJITAS WITH SWEET ONION

SERVES 4

▲ 1 large Vidalia onion, cut into ¾-inch-thick slices

▲ 2 red bell peppers, stems and seeds discarded, peppers quartered

1 teaspoon chili powder

1 teaspoon ground cumin

½ teaspoon kosher salt

¼ teaspoon black pepper

1 pound skirt steak, trimmed

4 (10-inch) whole wheat flour tortillas, warmed

▲ 1½ cups shredded romaine lettuce

▲ 1 large tomato, diced

▲ 3 tablespoons fat-free sour cream

2 tablespoons chopped fresh cilantro

Lime wedges

❶ Spray grill rack with nonstick spray; preheat grill to medium-high or prepare medium-hot fire. Generously coat onion slices and bell peppers with olive oil nonstick spray. Place on grill rack and grill, turning once or twice, until softened and browned, about 8 minutes. Transfer to cutting board.

❷ Meanwhile, combine chili powder, cumin, salt, and black pepper in small bowl. Sprinkle mixture over both sides of steak. Place steak on grill rack and grill until instant-read thermometer inserted into side of steak registers 145°F for medium, 3–4 minutes on each side. Transfer steak to cutting board and loosely cover with foil; let stand 3 minutes. Cut steak across grain into 12 slices. Cut onion and bell peppers into strips.

❸ Layer each tortilla with 3 slices steak and top each evenly with onion, bell peppers, lettuce, tomato, sour cream, and cilantro. Serve with lime wedges.

PER SERVING (1 filled tortilla): 374 Cal, 12 g Total Fat, 3 g Sat Fat, 0 g Trans Fat, 51 mg Chol, 507 mg Sod, 34 g Carb, 6 g Sugar, 5 g Fib, 29 g Prot, 54 mg Calc.

9 PointsPlus® value

CARNE ASADA TACOS

SERVES 4

¼ cup lime juice

2 tablespoons orange juice

1 tablespoon white vinegar

1 teaspoon olive oil

4 garlic cloves, minced

▲ 1 jalapeño pepper, seeded and minced

▲ 1 pound lean boneless sirloin steak, trimmed

¼ teaspoon kosher salt

½ teaspoon black pepper

4 (7-inch) whole wheat flour tortillas, warmed

▲ 1 cup prepared refrigerated pico de gallo

❶ Combine lime juice, orange juice, vinegar, oil, garlic, and jalapeño in large zip-close plastic bag; add steak. Squeeze out air and seal bag; turn to coat steak. Refrigerate 10 minutes.

❷ Spray ridged grill pan with nonstick spray; set over medium-high heat until very hot.

❸ Remove steak from marinade; discard marinade. Pat steak dry with paper towels and sprinkle with salt and pepper. Place steak in pan and grill until instant-read thermometer inserted into side of steak registers 145°F for medium, about 6 minutes on each side. Transfer steak to cutting board and loosely cover with foil; let stand 3 minutes. Cut steak across grain on diagonal into 12 thin slices; serve in tortillas with pico de gallo.

PER SERVING (3 slices steak, 1 tortilla, and 2 tablespoons pico de gallo): 268 Cal, 9 g Total Fat, 2 g Sat Fat, 0 g Trans Fat, 49 mg Chol, 761 mg Sod, 23 g Carb, 4 g Sugar, 10 g Fib, 33 g Prot, 27 mg Calc.

FYI

The marinated beef dish known in Mexico as *carne asada* ("grilled meat" in Spanish) is sometimes eaten by itself but is also a popular filling for tacos and burritos.

PORK AND GREEN CHILE POSOLE STEW

SERVES 6

1   tablespoon canola oil

▲ 1¼ pounds boneless lean center cut
      pork loin, trimmed and cut into
      ¾-inch cubes

   ¼ teaspoon salt

▲ 1 onion, diced

▲ 2 carrots, diced

▲ 1 celery stalk, thinly sliced

   3 garlic cloves, minced

   1 tablespoon ground cumin

▲ 1 cup reduced-sodium chicken broth

▲ 1 (14½-ounce) can no-salt-added
      diced tomatoes

   1 (8-ounce) jar mild green taco sauce
      (such as Ortega)

▲ 1 (15-ounce) can yellow or white hominy,
      rinsed and drained

   ½ cup chopped fresh cilantro

❶ Heat oil in large saucepan over medium-high heat. Sprinkle pork with salt. Add half of pork to pan and cook, stirring frequently, until browned, about 3 minutes. Transfer pork to medium bowl with slotted spoon; repeat with remaining pork.

❷ Add onion to pan and cook until softened, about 3 minutes. Stir in carrots and celery; cook, stirring occasionally, until vegetables are browned, about 4 minutes. Add garlic and cumin and cook, stirring, 30 seconds.

❸ Stir in broth, scraping any browned bits from bottom of pan with spoon. Stir in tomatoes, taco sauce, hominy, and pork. Bring to boil; reduce heat and simmer, uncovered, until pork is cooked through and stew is thickened, about 10 minutes. Stir in cilantro.

PER SERVING (1 generous cup): 267 Cal, 9 g Total Fat, 2 g Sat Fat, 0 g Trans Fat, 66 mg Chol, 397 mg Sod, 20 g Carb, 6 g Sugar, 4 g Fib, 24 g Prot, 65 mg Calc.

TOSTADOS WITH PORK AND CHIPOTLE CREAM

SERVES 4

- ▲ 1 **(1-pound) pork tenderloin, trimmed**
- 1 **teaspoon chili powder**
- ⅛ **teaspoon kosher salt**
- ⅛ **teaspoon cinnamon**
- ▲ ½ **cup fat-free sour cream**
- 1 **teaspoon minced chipotle en adobo**
- 1 **tablespoon lime juice**
- ½ **teaspoon sugar**
- ▲ 1 **cup fat-free canned refried beans, warmed**
- 4 **(6-inch) corn tostada shells, warmed**
- ▲ 2 **cups sliced romaine lettuce**
- ▲ 1 **large tomato, chopped**

① Cut pork tenderloin into 4 equal pieces. Slice each horizontally at middle without cutting entirely through meat and open up each like a book. Combine chili powder, salt, and cinnamon in small bowl. Sprinkle onto pork, coating all sides.

② Spray large nonstick skillet with nonstick spray and set over medium-high heat. Add pork and cook, turning once, until browned and cooked through, about 10 minutes. Transfer to cutting board and let stand 3 minutes; cut into strips.

③ Combine sour cream, chipotle, lime juice, and sugar in small bowl. Spread warmed refried beans on tostados. Top with lettuce, strips of pork, and tomato; drizzle chipotle cream sauce evenly over top of each.

PER SERVING (1 tostada with 2 tablespoons cream): 284 Cal, 6 g Total Fat, 2 g Sat Fat, 1 g Trans Fat, 65 mg Chol, 550 mg Sod, 27 g Carb, 3 g Sugar, 5 g Fib, 28 g Prot, 101 mg Calc.

7 PointsPlus® value

TOMATILLO ENCHILADAS WITH GRILLED CHICKEN

SERVES 6

▲ 1 onion, chopped

4 garlic cloves, minced

▲ 1 jalapeño pepper, seeded and diced

1 teaspoon ground cumin

⅛ teaspoon salt

▲ 2 pounds tomatillos, husks removed, fruits rinsed and coarsely chopped

2 tablespoons water

▲ ¾ pound cooked grilled skinless boneless chicken breast, diced

▲ 1 cup fresh or thawed frozen corn kernels

▲ 1½ cups (6 ounces) shredded fat-free pepper Jack cheese

1 cup loosely packed fresh cilantro leaves

12 (6-inch) corn tortillas, warmed

① Preheat oven to 450°F. Spray large nonstick skillet with nonstick spray and set over medium-high heat. Add onion, garlic, and jalapeño and cook, stirring, until vegetables soften, 2–3 minutes. Stir in cumin and salt. Add tomatillos and water. Bring to boil; lower heat and simmer, uncovered, 7–8 minutes.

② Meanwhile, stir together chicken, corn, and 1 cup Jack cheese in large bowl.

③ Remove tomatillo sauce from heat and stir in cilantro. In two batches, transfer sauce to blender and puree, starting on low speed and holding blender lid down with folded kitchen towel. Stir 1 cup of sauce into chicken mixture; return remaining sauce to skillet.

④ Spread 1 cup tomatillo sauce in bottom of 9 x 13-inch baking dish. Dip 1 tortilla at a time in remaining sauce, place on cutting board, and fill with ⅓ cup chicken mixture. Roll up and place seam side down in dish. Repeat with remaining tortillas and chicken mixture. Spoon remaining sauce over enchiladas; sprinkle with remaining ½ cup cheese. Cover with foil and bake until heated through, 12–15 minutes. Remove foil, turn on broiler and broil enchiladas until cheese is browned, about 1 minute.

PER SERVING (2 enchiladas): 335 Cal, 6 g Total Fat, 1 g Sat Fat, 0 g Trans Fat, 51 mg Chol, 384 mg Sod, 41 g Carb, 9 g Sugar, 6 g Fib, 29 g Prot, 433 mg Calc.

8 PointsPlus® value

CHICKEN MOLE WITH YELLOW RICE

SERVES 4

▲ ¾ cup quick-cooking brown rice

¼ teaspoon ground turmeric

4 (3½-ounce) skinless boneless chicken thighs, trimmed

¼ teaspoon salt

3 garlic cloves, minced

1 tablespoon chili powder

1 teaspoon ground cumin

½ teaspoon cinnamon

▲ 1 (8-ounce) can tomato sauce

▲ ½ cup reduced-sodium chicken broth

1 ounce semisweet chocolate, chopped

2 teaspoons reduced-fat peanut butter

❶ Cook rice according to package directions, omitting salt and fat, but adding turmeric.

❷ Meanwhile, spray nonstick skillet with nonstick spray and place over medium-high heat. Sprinkle chicken with salt and add to skillet. Cook, turning once, until browned, about 3 minutes per side. Transfer to plate.

❸ Return skillet to medium heat. Add garlic, chili powder, cumin, and cinnamon; cook, stirring, 30 seconds. Stir in tomato sauce, broth, chocolate, and peanut butter. Bring mixture to simmer, stirring occasionally. Reduce heat to medium-low and return chicken with accumulated juices to skillet. Turn to coat chicken with sauce and simmer until cooked through, 6–7 minutes. Serve with rice.

PER SERVING (1 chicken thigh, ⅓ cup sauce, and ½ cup rice): 283 Cal, 12 g Total Fat, 4 g Sat Fat, 0 g Trans Fat, 65 mg Chol, 556 mg Sod, 24 g Carb, 7 g Sugar, 3 g Fib, 22 g Prot, 42 mg Calc.

FYI

Steamed green beans and carrots make a healthful, colorful side dish for rich mole. Dress them with a little lime juice, if you like.

OURS vs. THEIRS

Mexican food seems to make any occasion a fiesta, even a casual weeknight meal. Cooking restaurant favorites at home can be surprisingly easy and affordable, and you'll enjoy some very satisfying *PointsPlus* value savings too. Here are a few examples to savor:

YOUR CHOICE	OURS	THEIRS	WITH YOUR SAVINGS TRY
GUACAMOLE	A serving of our Enlightened Guacamole with Jicama Dipping Sticks, p. 88: **3 *PointsPlus* value**	¼-cup serving of restaurant-style guacamole and 1¼ ounces of tortilla chips: **7 *PointsPlus* value**	A (12-ounce) bottle of light beer: **4 *PointsPlus* value**
TOSTADO	One of our Tostados with Pork and Chipotle, p. 92: **7 *PointsPlus* value**	An 8¼-ounce restaurant beef tostada: **11 *PointsPlus* value**	1 cup (2 scoops) mango sorbet: **4 *PointsPlus* value**
ENCHILADAS	Two of our Tomatillo Enchiladas with Grilled Chicken, p. 94: **8 *PointsPlus* value**	Two restaurant-style chicken enchiladas (10 ½ ounces): **11 *PointsPlus* value**	A serving of our Ceviche-Style Shrimp Salad with Mango and Avocado, p. 87: **3 *PointsPlus* value**
TAMALE PIE	One of our Tamale Pot Pies with Turkey and Pepper Jack, p. 99: **6 *PointsPlus* value**	1 cup restaurant-style tamale pie: **12 *PointsPlus* value**	1½ cups gazpacho: **6 *PointsPlus* value**
QUESADILLA	One of our Mushroom and Goat Cheese Quesadillas, p. 105: **6 *PointsPlus* value**	1 (6-inch) restaurant cheese quesadilla: **12 *PointsPlus* value**	¾ cup refried beans: **6 *PointsPlus* value**

CHICKEN CHALUPAS WITH GOAT CHEESE

SERVES 4

▲ 1   pound ground skinless chicken breast

½   teaspoon canola oil

▲ 1   onion, chopped

3   garlic cloves, minced

1   tablespoon chopped fresh oregano
     or 1 teaspoon dried

2   teaspoons chili powder

▲ 1   (15-ounce) can no-salt-added pinto
     beans, rinsed and drained

▲ 1   (14½-ounce) can no-salt-added
     diced tomatoes

▲ 1   (8-ounce) can no-salt-added
     tomato sauce

▲ 1   (4¼-ounce) can mild green chiles,
     drained

8   (6-inch) whole wheat flour tortillas,
     warmed

½   cup (2 ounces) crumbled goat cheese

❶ Spray large nonstick skillet with nonstick spray and set over medium-high heat. Add chicken and cook, breaking up chunks with side of wooden spoon, until browned, about 4 minutes. Transfer to bowl.

❷ Heat oil in skillet; add onion and cook, stirring frequently, until softened, about 4 minutes. Add garlic, oregano, and chili powder; cook 30 seconds. Stir in beans, diced tomatoes, tomato sauce, and green chiles. Bring to boil; lower heat to medium-low and stir in chicken. Simmer, uncovered, until slightly thickened, about 6 minutes.

❸ Place 2 tortillas on each of 4 plates. Divide chicken mixture among tortillas and sprinkle evenly with goat cheese.

PER SERVING (2 tortillas, ¾ cup chicken filling, and 2 tablespoons cheese): 458 Cal, 12 g Total Fat, 3 g Sat Fat, 0 g Trans Fat, 69 mg Chol, 850 mg Sod, 58 g Carb, 9 g Sugar, 27 g Fib, 46 g Prot, 138 mg Calc.

FYI

A refreshing chopped salad of cucumbers, jicama, tomatoes, and endive dressed with lemon juice makes a crisp accompaniment to chalupas.

TAMALE POT PIES WITH TURKEY AND PEPPER JACK

SERVES 6

- ▲ 1¼ pounds ground skinless turkey breast
- ▲ 1 onion, chopped
- ▲ 1 (10-ounce) can diced tomatoes with green chiles
- ▲ 1 (8-ounce) can no-salt-added tomato sauce
- ▲ 1 cup fresh or frozen thawed corn kernels
-    1 tablespoon ground cumin
- ▲ ¾ cup yellow cornmeal
-    ¼ teaspoon salt
-    3 cups cold water
- ▲ ¾ cup (3 ounces) shredded fat-free pepper Jack cheese

1 Preheat oven to 400°F. Spray 6 (8-ounce) ramekins or baking dishes with nonstick spray.

2 Spray large nonstick skillet with nonstick spray and set over high heat. Add turkey and onion and cook, breaking up chunks of turkey with side of wooden spoon, until turkey is no longer pink, 5–6 minutes. Stir in diced tomatoes with juices, tomato sauce, corn, and cumin. Divide mixture evenly among ramekins.

3 Whisk together cornmeal, salt, and ¾ cup of water in medium bowl. Bring remaining 2¼ cups water to boil in medium saucepan over high heat; slowly whisk cornmeal mixture into boiling water. Reduce heat and simmer, stirring frequently, until thickened, 4–5 minutes. Remove from heat and stir in ½ cup Jack cheese.

4 Spoon cornmeal mixture evenly on top of turkey. Place ramekins on baking sheet and bake 8 minutes. Sprinkle remaining ¼ cup cheese evenly over tops and bake until mixture is bubbly and cheese is melted, about 5 minutes.

PER SERVING (1 pot pie): 251 Cal, 2 g Total Fat, 0 g Sat Fat, 0 g Trans Fat, 39 mg Chol, 296 mg Sod, 29 g Carb, 6 g Sugar, 3 g Fib, 31 g Prot, 224 mg Calc.

TURKEY PICADILLO WITH CILANTRO RICE

SERVES 4

¾ cups quick-cooking brown rice

1¼ pounds ground skinless turkey breast

1½ teaspoons canola oil

1 onion, chopped

1 cubanelle pepper, chopped

3 garlic cloves, minced

1 tablespoon chopped fresh oregano or 1 teaspoon dried

2 teaspoons ground cumin

¼ teaspoon red pepper flakes

1 (15-ounce) can no-salt-added tomato sauce

½ cup golden raisins

¼ cup chopped pitted green olives

½ cup loosely packed fresh cilantro leaves

3 tablespoons lime juice

1. Cook rice according to package directions, omitting any salt or fat.

2. Meanwhile, spray large nonstick skillet with nonstick spray and set over medium-high heat. Add turkey and cook, breaking up chunks with side of wooden spoon, until browned, about 6 minutes. Transfer to medium bowl.

3. Return skillet to medium-high heat and add oil. Add onion and cubanelle pepper and cook, stirring frequently, until vegetables soften, about 4 minutes. Add garlic, oregano, cumin, and pepper flakes and stir 1 minute. Stir in tomato sauce, raisins, olives, and turkey. Reduce heat to low; cover and simmer until flavors blend, about 5 minutes.

4. Place cilantro and lime juice in food processor; process until combined, about 1 minute. Stir cilantro mixture into cooked rice and serve alongside picadillo.

PER SERVING (1¼ cups picadillo and ½ cup rice): 380 Cal, 7 g Total Fat, 0 g Sat Fat, 0 g Trans Fat, 56 mg Chol, 326 mg Sod, 44 g Carb, 23 g Sugar, 5 g Fib, 39 g Prot, 70 mg Calc.

BAHIAN FISH STEW

SERVES 4

1½ teaspoons olive oil

▲ 1   Vidalia or other sweet onion, diced

▲ 1   red bell pepper, diced

▲ 1   large sweet potato, peeled and cut into ½-inch pieces

   3   garlic cloves, minced

   1   tablespoon finely grated peeled fresh ginger

▲ 1   cup reduced-sodium chicken broth

▲ 4   large plum tomatoes (about 1 pound), chopped

▲ 1¼ pounds mahimahi, striped bass, or other firm white fish, cut into 1½-inch chunks

   ½   cup light (reduced-fat) coconut milk

   1   tablespoon lemon juice

   3   tablespoons chopped fresh cilantro

Hot sauce for serving (optional)

❶ Heat oil in large nonstick skillet over medium-high heat. Add onion, bell pepper, and sweet potato; cook, stirring frequently, until onion and pepper are softened, about 5 minutes. Add garlic and ginger; cook, stirring, until fragrant, about 1 minute. Stir in broth. Cover, reduce heat to medium, and simmer 5 minutes.

❷ Stir in tomatoes, fish, and coconut milk. Cover and cook 5 minutes. Uncover and cook until fish is just opaque and sweet potatoes are tender, 3–5 minutes. Stir in lemon juice and cilantro. Serve with hot sauce, if desired.

PER SERVING (1¾ cups): 257 Cal, 5 g Total Fat, 1 g Sat Fat, 0 g Trans Fat, 103 mg Chol, 171 mg Sod, 23 g Carb, 10 g Sugar, 4 g Fib, 30 g Prot, 70 mg Calc.

FYI

This stew gets its culinary inspiration from the Brazil's coastal state of Bahia, where seafood is plentiful and coconut milk is a common ingredient. If you'd like a spicier stew, add a diced seeded chile to the skillet along with the garlic and ginger in Step 1.

FISH TACOS WITH TANGY CILANTRO SLAW

SERVES 4 • READY IN 20 MIN OR LESS

½   cup light sour cream

1   teaspoon minced chipotles en adobo

▲   2½ cups shredded red cabbage

▲   1   large carrot, shredded

▲   2   scallions, thinly sliced

½   cup chopped fresh cilantro

Zest and juice of 1 lime

2   teaspoons canola oil

½   teaspoon salt

▲   1   pound skinless cod or halibut fillet, cut into 1-inch pieces

½   teaspoon chili powder

8   (6-inch) corn tortillas, warmed

① Stir sour cream and chipotles en adobo together in small bowl.

② Stir cabbage, carrot, scallions, cilantro, lime zest and juice, oil, and ¼ teaspoon of salt together in large bowl.

③ Spray ridged grill pan with nonstick spray; set over medium-high heat until very hot.

④ Sprinkle fish with chili powder and remaining ¼ teaspoon salt. Place on grill pan and cook, turning once, until fish is just opaque throughout, about 3 minutes per side. Divide fish evenly among tortillas. Top evenly with slaw and sour cream mixture.

PER SERVING (2 tacos): 312 Cal, 9 g Total Fat, 2 g Sat Fat, 0 g Trans Fat, 54 mg Chol, 478 mg Sod, 30 g Carb, 4 g Fib, 22 g Prot, 87 mg Calc.

FYI

For even more healthy veggie crunch, add 1 cup shredded peeled jicama to the slaw in Step 2.

FISH TACOS WITH
TANGY CILANTRO SLAW

BAKED PLANTAINS WITH RICE AND BEANS

SERVES 6

2 green plantains, peeled and thinly sliced on the diagonal

¼ teaspoon kosher salt

2 teaspoons canola oil

▲ 1 small onion, diced

▲ 1 small red or green bell pepper, diced

▲ 1 jalapeño pepper, seeded and chopped

2 garlic cloves, minced

1 tablespoon chopped fresh oregano or 1 teaspoon dried

▲ 3 cups instant brown rice

▲ 1 (28-ounce) can red kidney beans, rinsed and drained

▲ 3 cups reduced-sodium chicken broth

▲ 6 radishes, thinly sliced

¼ cup lightly packed cilantro leaves

Lime wedges

❶ Preheat oven to 450°F. Line 2 baking sheets with foil. Arrange plantain slices in single layer on baking sheets; spray with nonstick spray. Turn slices and spray other side. Sprinkle salt on top. Bake until golden and crisp, about 20 minutes, turning once about halfway through baking.

❷ Meanwhile, heat oil in large saucepan over medium-high heat. Add onion, bell pepper, and jalapeño; cook, stirring, until softened, about 4 minutes. Stir in garlic and oregano. Stir in rice, beans, and broth; bring mixture to boil. Cover and reduce heat to medium-low; simmer until most liquid is absorbed and rice is soft, 15–20 minutes. Remove from heat and let stand, covered, 5 minutes.

❸ Divide rice and beans and plantains among 6 plates. Top rice and beans with radish slices and cilantro and serve with lime wedges.

PER SERVING (1⅓ cups rice and beans, 1 radish, and 8 plantain slices): 443 Cal, 5 g Total Fat, 0 g Sat Fat, 0 g Trans Fat, 0 mg Chol, 131 mg Sod, 86 g Carb, 13 g Sugar, 16 g Fib, 17 g Prot, 13 mg Calc.

MUSHROOM AND GOAT CHEESE QUESADILLAS

SERVES 4 • READY IN 20 MIN OR LESS

2 teaspoons olive oil

▲ 1 small Vidalia or other sweet onion, thinly sliced

▲ 1 jalapeño pepper, seeded and minced

▲ 1 (10-ounce) package sliced cremini mushrooms

▲ 1 (3½-ounce) package sliced shiitake mushrooms

¼ teaspoon salt

¼ teaspoon black pepper

2 tablespoons chopped fresh cilantro leaves

½ cup (2 ounces) crumbled reduced-fat goat cheese

¼ cup reduced-fat cream cheese, softened

4 (7-inch) whole wheat flour tortillas

▲ ½ cup fat-free salsa

❶ Heat oil in large nonstick skillet over medium-high heat. Add onion and jalapeño and cook, stirring frequently, until softened, about 4 minutes. Add mushrooms, salt, and black pepper; cook, stirring, until mushrooms are softened, 6–8 minutes. Remove from heat and stir in cilantro.

❷ Meanwhile, preheat broiler and spray large baking sheet with nonstick spray. Combine goat cheese and cream cheese in small bowl.

❸ Spread 1 tablespoon cheese mixture onto each tortilla. Spoon one fourth of mushroom mixture onto bottom half of each tortilla; fold top over filling. Place quesadillas on baking sheet. Broil until tops are browned, 1–2 minutes. Flip over and cook until browned and cheese is melted, 1–2 minutes. Serve with salsa.

PER SERVING (1 quesadilla and 2 tablespoons salsa): 213 Cal, 9 g Total Fat, 2 g Sat Fat, 0 g Trans Fat, 11 mg Chol, 679 mg Sod, 30 g Carb, 9 g Sugar, 11 g Fib, 13 g Prot, 73 mg Calc.

FYI

For extra veggie goodness, add a few cups of baby spinach to the skillet along with the mushrooms in Step 1.

CHAPTER 5

Treasures
of the
Mediterranean

Appetizers

GREEK SALAD WITH FETA AND ARTICHOKES

GARLICKY GREEK POTATO DIP (SKORDALIA)

Main Courses

MOUSSAKA IN MINUTES

TURKISH LAMB-AND-ZUCCHINI KEBABS OVER BULGUR

SOUVLAKI-STYLE PORK CHOPS WITH TZATZIKI

WINE-BRAISED CHICKEN WITH ARTICHOKES AND OLIVES

GRILLED CHICKEN GYROS WITH BELL PEPPER

TURKISH PITA PIZZA (LAHMACUN)

LEMON-OREGANO GRILLED MAHIMAHI AND SWEET ONIONS

SHRIMP SAGANAKI WITH FETA AND DILL

GREEK FISHERMEN'S POT

TURKISH BULGUR PILAF WITH VEGETABLES

TOMATO AND OKRA STEW WITH CHICKPEAS

Mediterranean Pantry Partners

KEEP THESE STAPLES ON HAND TO QUICKLY GET HEALTHFUL MEALS ON THE TABLE.

Artichoke Hearts ▲ Artichokes are a favorite Mediterranean vegetable, and prepared hearts are a quick and easy way to enjoy them in salads and other dishes. Use thawed frozen hearts or hearts canned in water rather than those packed in oil to reduce the fat grams in your dishes.

Bulgur Wheat ▲ This Middle Eastern staple is packed with fiber and protein, and since it's made from partially cooked wheat kernels, it cooks up more quickly than most whole grains. Bulgur is the classic grain to use in tabbouleh, but it's also excellent as a side dish or in soups, salads, and pilafs.

Feta Cheese Tangy, crumbly feta is a great way to bring instant Mediterranean flavor to everything from salads and sandwiches to casseroles. Greek feta is traditionally made with goat's or sheep's milk, although most feta available in U.S. markets is made from cow's milk.

Ground Allspice So named because it carries the aroma of several spices—cloves, pepper, cinnamon, and nutmeg—allspice is popular worldwide in both sweet and savory dishes. It's found in a number of Greek and Turkish classics, especially meat dishes.

Kalamata Olives The briny, dark-purple kalamata, named after the southern Greek city of Kalamata, is a classic Mediterranean olive. Purchase pitted ones to make prep even easier.

Oregano Pungent, lightly minty oregano is the go-to herb of Greek cooking, showing up in everything from beef and lamb to fish and tomato sauce. One teaspoon dried oregano is equivalent to about one tablespoon of chopped fresh oregano.

Pita Pita breads come with or without pockets. Choose pocket breads for stuffing like a sandwich, flatbreads for making wedges or quick pizza dishes. Serve whole wheat or whole-grain pitas to get the most nutrients and fiber in your diet.

Plain Fat-Free Greek Yogurt ▲ Greek yogurt has won a lot of fans for its thick, creamy texture and a flavor that is rich and mild even in fat-free versions. It's a natural for making simple sauces for Greek and Turkish dishes, or just serve a dollop with your dishes for a healthy calcium and protein boost.

Mediterranean Treasures

GREEK SALAD WITH FETA AND ARTICHOKES

SERVES 4 AS AN APPETIZER • READY IN 20 MIN OR LESS

- **1** garlic clove, halved
- **1** teaspoon grated lemon zest
- **3** tablespoons lemon juice
- **1** tablespoon olive oil
- **1** teaspoon dried oregano
- **¼** teaspoon salt
- **¼** teaspoon black pepper
- ▲ **4** cups sliced romaine lettuce
- ▲ **2** cups baby arugula leaves
- ▲ **1** (14-ounce) can quartered artichoke hearts in water, drained
- ▲ **1** large Kirby cucumber, halved lengthwise and sliced
- ▲ **1** small yellow or red bell pepper, quartered and sliced
- ▲ **1** cup grape tomatoes, halved
- ▲ **¼** cup sliced red onion
- **6** pitted kalamata olives, cut in slivers
- ▲ **½** cup crumbled fat-free feta cheese

Rub inside of large salad bowl with cut sides of garlic clove; discard garlic. Add lemon zest and juice, oil, oregano, salt, and pepper to bowl; whisk until blended. Add romaine, arugula, artichoke hearts, cucumber, bell pepper, tomatoes, onion, and olives and toss to coat. Sprinkle with feta and serve.

PER SERVING (2¼ cups salad and 2 tablespoons feta): 156 Cal, 5 g Total Fat, 1 g Sat Fat, 0 g Trans Fat, 2 mg Chol, 981 mg Sod, 20 g Carb, 4 g Sugar, 6 g Fib, 9 g Prot, 107 mg Calc.

FYI

Make this a satisfying main-dish salad by adding rinsed and drained canned cannellini beans; a ½ cup sprinkled over each serving will increase the *PointsPlus* value by **2**.

GARLICKY GREEK POTATO DIP
(SKORDALIA), PAGE 112

GREEK SALAD WITH
FETA AND ARTICHOKES

GARLICKY GREEK POTATO DIP (SKORDALIA)

SERVES 8 AS AN APPETIZER

▲ 1 pound Yukon Gold potatoes, peeled and cut into 1-inch chunks

1 day-old whole wheat sandwich roll (about 4-inch diameter), soaked in water until soft

4 garlic cloves

2 tablespoons olive oil

3 tablespoons lemon juice

2 tablespoons slivered blanched almonds

2 tablespoons capers, rinsed and drained

½ teaspoon salt

¼ teaspoon black pepper

3 tablespoons water

▲ 2 Kirby cucumbers, sliced

▲ 2 heads Belgium endive, separated into leaves

▲ 1 (1-pound) bag baby carrots

❶ Bring potatoes and enough cold water to cover to boil in medium saucepan over high heat. Reduce heat; cover and simmer until potatoes are tender, about 15 minutes. Drain in colander. Return potatoes to pan and mash with potato masher until smooth.

❷ Squeeze water from roll; place roll in food processor. Add garlic and puree. Add oil; pulse until blended. Add lemon juice, almonds, capers, salt, pepper, and water and pulse until almonds and capers are very finely chopped. Scrape into medium bowl and stir in potatoes. Serve with cucumbers, endive, and carrots for dipping.

PER SERVING (6 tablespoons dip and about 1½ cups vegetables): 153 Cal, 5 g Total Fat, 1 g Sat Fat, 0 g Trans Fat, 0 mg Chol, 294 mg Sod, 26 g Carb, 6 g Sugar, 8 g Fib, 6 g Prot, 118 mg Calc.

FYI

In Greece, skordalia is a popular accompaniment to batter-fried fish and vegetables; using it as a dip for fresh raw vegetables is our healthy alternative. You can also serve it with baked pita chips if you like. The flavor of the dip will fully develop with time; if you can, make it at least 2 hours and up to 2 days ahead and refrigerate.

MOUSSAKA IN MINUTES

SERVES 4

1 teaspoon olive oil

▲ 1 small (1-pound) eggplant, cut into ½-inch chunks

▲ 1 large onion, diced

▲ ½ pound ground lean beef (7% fat or less)

3 large garlic cloves, minced

▲ 1 (14½-ounce) can fire-roasted diced tomatoes

▲ 1 (8-ounce) can no-salt-added tomato sauce

2½ teaspoons dried oregano

½ teaspoon ground allspice

½ teaspoon ground cinnamon

½ teaspoon black pepper

Pinch salt

▲ 1 cup fat-free ricotta cheese

▲ 1 large egg

▲ ¼ cup crumbled fat-free feta cheese

❶ Heat oil in large nonstick ovenproof skillet over medium-high heat. Add eggplant and onion; cover and cook, stirring occasionally, until vegetables are softened and lightly browned, 6–8 minutes. Transfer mixture to medium bowl.

❷ Add beef and garlic to skillet. Cook, breaking beef up with side of wooden spoon, until no longer pink, about 3 minutes.

❸ Return eggplant mixture to skillet. Add diced tomatoes, tomato sauce, oregano, allspice, cinnamon, pepper, and salt and bring to simmer. Reduce heat; cover and simmer, stirring occasionally, until eggplant is tender, about 5 minutes.

❹ Meanwhile, preheat broiler. Stir together ricotta, egg, and feta in small bowl. When eggplant is tender, spoon ricotta mixture over top and spread evenly (mixture will not completely cover top). Broil until topping is puffed and browned in spots, about 5 minutes.

PER SERVING (1¼ cups): 251 Cal, 6 g Total Fat, 2 g Sat Fat, 0 g Trans Fat, 94 mg Chol, 471 mg Sod, 26 g Carb, 13 g Sugar, 8 g Fib, 26 g Prot, 298 mg Calc.

6 PointsPlus® value

Mediterranean Treasures

TURKISH LAMB-AND-ZUCCHINI KEBABS OVER BULGUR

SERVES 4

▲ 1 (14½-ounce) can reduced-sodium chicken broth

¼ cup water

2 large garlic cloves, minced

▲ 1 cup bulgur

2 teaspoons olive oil

1½ teaspoons dried oregano

¾ teaspoon paprika

½ teaspoon salt

¾ pound boneless leg of lamb, trimmed and cut into 1-inch chunks

▲ 2 medium zucchini, halved lengthwise and cut into 1-inch pieces

▲ 2 large tomatoes, diced

3 tablespoons chopped fresh dill

2 teaspoons lemon juice

Fresh oregano leaves for garnish (optional)

❶ Spray grill rack with nonstick spray; preheat grill to medium or prepare medium fire.

❷ Meanwhile, combine broth, water, and 1 clove garlic in medium saucepan over high heat; bring to boil. Stir in bulgur. Reduce heat; cover and simmer until water is absorbed and bulgur is tender, about 12 minutes.

❸ Whisk together remaining garlic clove, 1 teaspoon oil, and dried oregano in large bowl. Whisk in paprika and salt. Add lamb and zucchini and toss to coat. Thread lamb and zucchini alternately onto 8 (8-inch) metal skewers. Place skewers on grill rack and grill, turning often, until lamb is browned and cooked through, about 10 minutes for medium.

❹ Meanwhile, toss together tomatoes, dill, lemon juice, and remaining 1 teaspoon oil in medium bowl. Divide bulgur among 4 plates and top each with 2 kebab skewers. Spoon tomato mixture over kebabs. Sprinkle with fresh oregano, if using.

PER SERVING (2 skewers, ¾ cup bulgur, and ¾ cup tomato salad): 378 Cal, 13 g Total Fat, 5 g Sat Fat, 0 g Trans Fat, 89 mg Chol, 414 mg Sod, 36 g Carb, 4 g Sugar, 9 g Fib, 32 g Prot, 62 mg Calc.

SOUVLAKI-STYLE PORK CHOPS WITH TZATZIKI

SERVES 4

1 tablespoon lemon juice

1½ teaspoons dried oregano

3 garlic cloves, finely minced

1½ teaspoons olive oil

¾ teaspoon salt

▲ 4 (¼-pound) lean center-cut boneless pork loin chops, trimmed

▲ ¾ cup plain fat-free Greek yogurt

▲ 1 Kirby cucumber, diced

¼ cup chopped fresh mint leaves

1 tablespoon water

1½ teaspoons red wine vinegar

▲ 6 ounces mixed baby greens

1 Combine lemon juice, oregano, 2 garlic cloves, 1 teaspoon oil, and ½ teaspoon salt in zip-close plastic bag; add pork. Squeeze out air and seal bag; turn to coat pork. Refrigerate, turning bag once or twice, 10 minutes.

2 Meanwhile, to make tzatziki, stir together yogurt, cucumber, mint, water, vinegar, remaining garlic clove, remaining ½ teaspoon oil, and remaining ¼ teaspoon salt.

3 Spray nonstick ridged grill pan with nonstick spray and set over medium heat. Place pork chops in pan and grill until instant-read thermometer inserted in center of chops registers 145°F, about 4 minutes on each side. Evenly divide greens among 4 plates. Top each serving with pork chop and ¼ cup tzatziki.

PER SERVING (1 pork chop, 2 cups greens, and ¼ cup tzatziki): 202 Cal, 8 g Total Fat, 2 g Sat Fat, 0 g Trans Fat, 66 mg Chol, 513 mg Sod, 7 g Carb, 4 g Sugar, 2 g Fib, 26 g Prot, 76 mg Calc.

FYI

Souvlaki means "little sword" in Greek (referring to the skewer it is traditionally cooked on). We've streamlined the preparation by eliminating the skewers, then paired our version with a quick tzatziki sauce.

WINE-BRAISED CHICKEN WITH ARTICHOKES AND OLIVES

SERVES 4 • READY IN 20 MIN OR LESS

3 tablespoons all-purpose flour

¼ teaspoon salt

¼ teaspoon black pepper

▲ 4 (5-ounce) skinless boneless chicken
   breasts

1½ teaspoons olive oil

3 large shallots, thinly sliced

½ cup dry white wine

▲ 1 (14½-ounce) can reduced-sodium
   chicken broth

▲ 1 (9-ounce) package frozen artichoke
   hearts, thawed

8 pitted kalamata olives, halved

2 teaspoons chopped fresh rosemary

2 tablespoons chopped fresh parsley

❶ Combine 2 tablespoons flour, salt, and pepper on large plate. Coat chicken breasts, one at a time, in mixture.

❷ Heat oil in large nonstick skillet over medium-high heat. Add chicken; scatter shallots around chicken. Cook, turning chicken once and stirring shallots occasionally, until chicken is lightly browned, about 5 minutes.

❸ Stir in wine. Cook, scraping up browned bits from bottom of skillet, about 30 seconds. Add broth. Sprinkle remaining 1 tablespoon flour over broth and whisk in. Bring to boil. Add artichoke hearts, olives, and rosemary. Reduce heat and simmer, uncovered, stirring sauce occasionally, until chicken is cooked through, about 4 minutes.

❹ Transfer chicken to platter. Continue to simmer sauce until reduced and thickened, about 3 minutes. Spoon sauce over chicken and sprinkle with parsley.

PER SERVING (1 piece chicken and ½ cup sauce): 298 Cal, 9 g Total Fat, 2 g Sat Fat, 0 g Trans Fat, 78 mg Chol, 412 mg Sod, 16 g Carb, 1 g Sugar, 4 g Fib, 34 g Prot, 65 mg Calc.

8 PointsPlus® value

GRILLED CHICKEN GYROS
WITH BELL PEPPER

GRILLED CHICKEN GYROS WITH BELL PEPPER

SERVES 4 • READY IN 20 MIN OR LESS

▲ 1 **large red bell pepper, quartered**

2 **teaspoons olive oil**

1 **large garlic clove, minced**

1 **teaspoon ground cumin**

1 **teaspoon dried oregano**

¼ **teaspoon salt**

¼ **teaspoon cayenne pepper**

▲ 4 **(¼-pound) thin-sliced skinless chicken cutlets**

4 **(7-inch) whole wheat pocketless pita breads, warmed**

▲ 1 **large Kirby cucumber, halved lengthwise, sliced**

▲ ½ **small red onion, sliced**

▲ ½ **cup plain fat-free Greek yogurt**

① Spray nonstick ridged grill pan with canola nonstick spray; set over medium heat. Place bell pepper in pan and grill, turning occasionally, until tender and browned, about 10 minutes.

② Meanwhile, whisk together oil, garlic, cumin, oregano, salt, and cayenne in large bowl. Add chicken and turn to coat. Transfer chicken to pan and grill, turning once, until chicken is browned and cooked through, 5–6 minutes.

③ Transfer bell pepper and chicken to cutting board and cut into strips. Top pitas evenly with chicken, bell pepper, cucumber, onion, and yogurt. Roll up pitas and serve immediately.

PER SERVING (1 filled pita): 236 Cal, 5 g Total Fat, 1 g Sat Fat, 0 g Trans Fat, 0 mg Chol, 501 mg Sod, 42 g Carb, 5 g Sugar, 7 g Fib, 10 g Prot, 53 mg Calc.

6
PointsPlus®
value
™

Mediterranean Treasures

OURS vs. THEIRS

We can't resist these recipes for healthful Greek and Turkish favorites. Our aim is to give you big flavor and filling portions while helping you stay within your daily *PointsPlus* Target. Here's how some of the recipes in this chapter match up against versions you might find at your local Mediterranean restaurant.

YOUR CHOICE	OURS	THEIRS	WITH YOUR SAVINGS TRY
GREEK SALAD	A serving of our Greek Salad with Feta and Artichokes, p. 110: *4 PointsPlus* value	3 cups restaurant-style Greek salad with dressing: *10 PointsPlus* value	1½ cups avgolemono soup: *6 PointsPlus* value
MOUSSAKA	A serving of our Moussaka in Minutes, p. 113: *6 PointsPlus* value	3 x 4-inch piece of restaurant-style moussaka: *12 PointsPlus* value	A (4-ounce) glass red wine and 12 large olives: *6 PointsPlus* value total
SOUVLAKI	A serving of our Souvlaki-Style Pork Chops with Tzatziki, p. 116: *5 PointsPlus* value	6½-ounce restaurant-style chicken souvlaki in pita bread: *8 PointsPlus* value	1 cup plain Greek fat-free yogurt with fresh figs: *3 PointsPlus* value
GYRO	One of our Grilled Chicken Gyros with Bell Pepper, p. 119: *6 PointsPlus* value	11-ounce restaurant-style gyro: *16 PointsPlus* value	A serving of our Garlicky Greek Potato Dip (Skordalia), p. 112, and ½ cup tabbouleh: *10 PointsPlus* value total

TURKISH PITA PIZZA (LAHMACUN)

SERVES 4 • READY IN 20 MIN OR LESS

▲ 1   large red onion, halved and sliced

▲ ¾   pound ground skinless turkey breast

3   large garlic cloves, minced

1¼ teaspoons ground cumin

1   teaspoon paprika

½   teaspoon salt

¼   teaspoon ground allspice

¼   teaspoon ground cinnamon

1   tablespoon tomato paste

2   tablespoons water

4   (7-inch) whole wheat pocketless
    pita breads

▲ 1   large tomato, diced

1   cup fresh mint or parsley leaves

❶ Heat oven to 475°F; spray 2 baking sheets with nonstick spray.

❷ Spray large nonstick skillet with nonstick spray and set over medium-high heat. Add 1 cup onion and cook, stirring frequently, until golden, about 5 minutes. Add turkey, garlic, cumin, paprika, salt, allspice, and cinnamon. Cook, breaking up turkey with side of wooden spoon, until turkey is no longer pink, about 4 minutes. Stir in tomato paste and water; remove from heat.

❸ Place pitas on baking sheets and top each evenly with turkey mixture. Bake until undersides are crisp, about 8 minutes. Top each with remaining onion, tomato, and mint.

PER SERVING (1 pizza): 301 Cal, 3 g Total Fat, 0 g Sat Fat, 0 g Trans Fat, 34 mg Chol, 721 mg Sod, 44 g Carb, 4 g Sugar, 7 g Fib, 29 g Prot, 53 mg Calc.

FYI

Lahmacun means "dough with meat" in Turkish, and it's a popular fast food in many Middle Eastern countries. Typically, the pita is rolled up for easy eating, but you can also cut it into wedges like a pizza or eat it with a knife and fork.

LEMON-OREGANO GRILLED MAHIMAHI AND SWEET ONIONS

SERVES 4

Zest and juice of 1 lemon

1   **tablespoon olive oil**

2   **tablespoons chopped fresh oregano or 2 teaspoons dried**

1   **garlic clove, minced**

¾   **teaspoon salt**

½   **teaspoon black pepper**

▲ 4   **(6-ounce) mahimahi fillets**

▲ 1   **medium sweet onion, cut into ½-inch-thick slices**

1   **lemon, cut into 4 wedges**

❶ Spray grill rack with nonstick spray. Preheat grill to medium-high or prepare medium-hot fire.

❷ Combine lemon zest and juice, oil, oregano, garlic, ½ teaspoon of salt, and ¼ teaspoon of pepper in shallow bowl. Add mahimahi and turn to coat. Let stand at room temperature 10 minutes.

❸ Lightly spray onion slices with nonstick spray and sprinkle with remaining ¼ teaspoon salt and remaining ¼ teaspoon pepper. Place onions and mahimahi on grill rack. Grill, turning once, until mahimahi is just opaque in center and onions are tender, 8–10 minutes.

❹ During the last 5 minutes of cooking, add lemon wedges to grill and cook until lightly charred, about 5 minutes. Divide fish, onions, and lemon wedges among 4 plates.

PER SERVING (1 mahimahi fillet, ⅓ cup grilled onions, and 1 lemon wedge): 163 Cal, 1 g Total Fat, 0 g Sat Fat, 0 g Trans Fat, 124 mg Chol, 588 mg Sod, 5 g Carb, 3 g Sugar, 1 g Fib, 32 g Prot, 50 mg Calc.

SHRIMP SAGANAKI WITH FETA AND DILL

SERVES 4 • READY IN 20 MIN OR LESS

1½ teaspoons olive oil

▲ 1 large onion, chopped

½ cup dry white wine

3 large garlic cloves, minced

▲ 1 (14½-ounce) can fire-roasted diced tomatoes

¼ teaspoon red pepper flakes

▲ 1 pound large shrimp, peeled and deveined

¼ cup crumbled reduced-fat feta

¼ cup chopped fresh dill

▲ 2 cups cooked brown rice

1 Heat oil in large nonstick skillet over medium-high heat. Add onion; cook, stirring frequently, until golden, about 5 minutes. Stir in wine and garlic and simmer 1 minute. Add tomatoes and pepper flakes; bring to boil. Reduce heat and simmer, uncovered, 3 minutes.

2 Add shrimp and simmer over medium-low heat, stirring often, until shrimp are just opaque in center, about 4 minutes. Remove from heat. Stir in feta and dill and let stand until feta softens slightly, about 1 minute. Spoon ½ cup brown rice onto each of 4 plates; top rice evenly with shrimp and sauce.

PER SERVING (1 cup shrimp and sauce and ½ cup rice): 294 Cal, 5 g Total Fat, 1 g Sat Fat, 0 g Trans Fat, 171 mg Chol, 543 mg Sod, 33 g Carb, 5 g Sugar, 3 g Fib, 23 g Prot, 98 mg Calc.

8 PointsPlus® value

FYI

Shrimp and brown rice make this variation of Greece's famous *saganaki* cheese dish a healthful meal. Try serving it with a side of steamed spinach sprinkled with lemon juice.

GREEK FISHERMEN'S POT

SERVES 4 • READY IN 20 MIN OR LESS

1½ teaspoons olive oil

▲ 1 fennel bulb, trimmed and sliced, fronds reserved for garnish

▲ 1 large leek, thinly sliced (white and light green parts only), and rinsed well

3 large garlic cloves, minced

▲ 1 (14½-ounce) can diced tomatoes in juice

1 cup dry white wine

1 (8-ounce) bottle clam juice

1 tablespoon chopped fresh thyme or 1 teaspoon dried

¼ teaspoon salt

¼ teaspoon black pepper

▲ 1 pound mussels, scrubbed and debearded

▲ ½ pound sea scallops

▲ ½ pound skinless cod fillet, cut into 1½-inch chunks

❶ Heat olive oil in large deep skillet over medium-high heat. Add fennel, leek, and garlic. Cook, stirring occasionally, until vegetables soften, about 6 minutes. Add tomatoes, wine, clam juice, thyme, salt, and pepper and bring to boil. Reduce heat and simmer 3 minutes for flavors to blend.

❷ Add mussels, scallops, and cod. Reduce heat; cover and simmer, stirring gently once or twice, until mussels open and scallops and cod are just opaque in center, about 5 minutes.

❸ Discard any mussels that do not open. Divide stew among 4 bowls. Chop reserved fennel fronds and sprinkle over each serving.

PER SERVING (2½ cups): 230 Cal, 3 g Total Fat, 0 g Sat Fat, 0 g Trans Fat, 49 mg Chol, 776 mg Sod, 16 g Carb, 4 g Sugar, 2 g Fib, 24 g Prot, 133 mg Calc.

FYI

Feel free to substitute any thick, white-fleshed fish fillet for the cod. Sea bass and halibut are good alternatives.

GREEK FISHERMEN'S POT

TURKISH BULGUR PILAF WITH VEGETABLES

SERVES 4

2   teaspoons olive oil

▲ 1   onion, diced

▲ 1   red or yellow bell pepper, diced

▲ 1   small (1-pound) eggplant, diced

▲ 1   zucchini, quartered lengthwise and thinly sliced

2   garlic cloves, minced

¾   teaspoon ground cumin

⅛   teaspoon cayenne pepper, or more to taste

3   tablespoons tomato paste

▲ 2   cups reduced-sodium chicken broth

▲ ⅔   cup bulgur

⅓   cup chopped fresh flat-leaf parsley or mint

❶ Heat oil in large nonstick skillet over medium-high heat. Add onion and bell pepper. Cook, stirring frequently, until vegetables soften, about 3 minutes. Add eggplant and zucchini and cook, stirring occasionally, until eggplant and zucchini soften, about 3 minutes.

❷ Add garlic, cumin, and cayenne. Cook, stirring, until fragrant, about 30 seconds. Stir in tomato paste. Stir in broth and bring to boil. Stir in bulgur. Reduce heat; cover and simmer, until vegetables and bulgur are tender and liquid is absorbed, about 12 minutes. Remove from heat and stir in parsley.

PER SERVING (1¼ cups): 191 Cal, 4 g Total Fat, 1 g Sat Fat, 0 g Trans Fat, 0 mg Chol, 150 mg Sod, 35 g Carb, 9 g Sugar, 11 g Fib, 8 g Prot, 60 mg Calc.

FYI

Yogurt is a delicious, refreshing topping for this dish. A ⅓-cup dollop of plain fat-free Greek yogurt on each serving will increase the *PointsPlus* value by *1*.

TOMATO AND OKRA STEW WITH CHICKPEAS

SERVES 4 • READY IN 20 MIN OR LESS

1½ teaspoons olive oil

▲ 1 large onion, diced

▲ 1 pound fresh okra, cut into ½-inch rounds or 1 (16-ounce) bag frozen cut okra, thawed

4 large garlic cloves, minced

▲ 1 cup grape tomatoes, halved

▲ 1 (15-ounce) can chickpeas, rinsed and drained

▲ 1 (8-ounce) can tomato sauce

½ teaspoon salt

¼ teaspoon red pepper flakes

1 teaspoon grated lemon zest

3 tablespoons chopped fresh dill

1 Heat oil in large nonstick skillet over medium-high heat. Add onion and cook, stirring frequently, until golden, about 5 minutes. Stir in okra. Cook, stirring frequently, until okra softens, about 3 minutes. Stir in garlic; then stir in tomatoes, chickpeas, tomato sauce, salt, and pepper flakes. Simmer, uncovered, until vegetables are tender, about 5 minutes.

2 Remove from heat and stir in lemon zest and dill.

PER SERVING (1½ cups): 175 Cal, 3 g Total Fat, 0 g Sat Fat, 0 g Trans Fat, 0 mg Chol, 692 mg Sod, 31 g Carb, 8 g Sugar, 9 g Fib, 8 g Prot, 136 mg Calc.

4 PointsPlus® value

Mediterranean Treasures

CHAPTER 6

Japanese Classics

Appetizers

GREEN SALAD WITH GINGER-CARROT VINAIGRETTE

MISO-MUSHROOM SOUP

Main Courses

FILET STEAKS WITH SESAME-WASABI BUTTER AND WATERCRESS

NEGAMAKI-STYLE BEEF AND GREEN BEAN ROLLS

PORK CHOPS TONKATSU

WARM UDON SALAD WITH SPICY PORK AND ASPARAGUS

CHICKEN AND VEGETABLE YAKITORI

HEARTY CHICKEN AND SOBA NOODLE SOUP

TUNA SASHIMI WITH DAIKON SALAD AND BROWN RICE

HALIBUT TERIYAKI WITH SESAME SNOW PEAS

SAKE-GRILLED JUMBO SHRIMP

SESAME TOFU AND EDAMAME STIR-FRY

GRILLED MISO-FLAVORED EGGPLANTS WITH ADZUKI BEAN SALAD

BROWN RICE GOMASIO WITH SHIITAKES AND TEMPEH

SCALLION EGGS WITH VEGETABLES AND TOFU

Japanese Pantry Partners

KEEP THESE STAPLES ON HAND TO QUICKLY GET HEALTHFUL MEALS ON THE TABLE.

Adzuki Beans ▲ These small, dark-red beans are extremely popular in Japanese cooking, both in savory dishes and in desserts. Like other legumes, they are rich in carbohydrates, dietary fiber, protein, and several vitamins and minerals.

Frozen Edamame ▲ These young, green soybeans are high in protein and fiber and great to have in your freezer. Use shelled frozen edamame in soups, salads, and stir-fries. Serve edamame beans in the pod as a quick snack.

Mirin Sweet, thick mirin is a Japanese rice wine used only for cooking. If you don't have it, you can make your own by combining 4 parts sake to 1 part sugar in a saucepan and simmering until the sugar is dissolved.

Miso Miso is a strong, salty paste made from fermented soybeans. The tan-color paste known as white miso is the mildest and most common in the United States.

Pickled Ginger This palette-cleansing condiment is made from sliced young ginger marinated in rice vinegar. It's a classic with sushi and sushimi, but also good for adding ginger flavor to dipping sauces.

Rice Vinegar Mellow and flavorful, rice vinegar is lower in acid than most other vinegars. If it's labeled "seasoned," it is made with the addition of salt and sugar.

Sake This Japanese wine is distilled from steamed rice and popular for drinking and for cooking. It's available dry and sweet; both types can be used for cooking. Good substitutes are dry sherry or white grape juice.

Sansho Also known as Szechuan pepper, this spice is ground to a very fine powder and adds an aromatic note to many Japanese dishes. Seek it out at spice stores or Asian markets, or substitute freshly ground black pepper.

Soba Noodles These hearty noodles are made from a combination of buckwheat and wheat flour; you can substitute whole wheat spaghetti or linguine if you like.

Togarashi This unique pepper blend is composed of ground red chile pepper, sesame seeds, roasted orange zest, fine pieces of seaweed, sansho pepper, and ginger. You can substitute cayenne pepper or hot paprika.

Udon Noodles These thick, white wheat noodles are very popular in Japan for soups. They are also commonly eaten cold in summer. Linguine is a good substitute for udon.

Wasabi This fiery green horseradish is available both as a powder, which you can mix with water to form a paste, or premixed in paste form. Most large supermarkets carry wasabi.

GREEN SALAD WITH GINGER-CARROT VINAIGRETTE

SERVES 4 AS AN APPETIZER • READY IN 20 MIN OR LESS

▲ 3 tablespoons finely grated carrot

1 teaspoon finely grated peeled fresh ginger

1½ tablespoons seasoned rice vinegar

2 teaspoons canola oil

1 teaspoon Asian (dark) sesame oil

½ teaspoon reduced-sodium soy sauce

1 tablespoon water

▲ 1 large head Boston lettuce, leaves torn

▲ 1 small Kirby cucumber, thinly sliced

▲ ½ cup cherry tomatoes, halved

▲ 2 scallions, thinly sliced

❶ Puree carrot, ginger, vinegar, canola oil, sesame oil, soy sauce, and water in blender or mini-food processor.

❷ Combine lettuce, cucumber, tomatoes, and scallions in large bowl. Drizzle with dressing and toss to coat.

PER SERVING (2 cups): 53 Cal, 4 g Total Fat, 0 g Sat Fat, 0 g Trans Fat, 0 mg Chol, 120 mg Sod, 5 g Carb, 3 g Sugar, 1 g Fib, 1 g Prot, 29 mg Calc.

2 PointsPlus value

MISO-MUSHROOM SOUP

SERVES 4 AS AN APPETIZER • READY IN 20 MIN OR LESS

▲ 2½ cups reduced-sodium chicken broth

▲ 8 shiitake mushrooms, stems discarded, caps thinly sliced

  ½ cup water

  1 tablespoon white miso

▲ ⅓ cup finely diced extra-firm tofu

▲ 16 snow peas, trimmed

▲ 2 scallions, thinly sliced

❶ Combine broth, mushrooms, and water in large saucepan and bring to boil over medium-high heat. Stir in miso, stirring until dissolved. Reduce heat and simmer until mushrooms are tender, about 3 minutes.

❷ Stir in tofu and cook until heated through, about 1 minute. Add snow peas and cook for 1 minute. Divide soup among 4 bowls, garnish with scallions, and serve.

PER SERVING (1 cup): 74 Cal, 2 g Total Fat, 0 g Sat Fat, 0 g Trans Fat, 0 mg Chol, 184 mg Sod, 10 g Carb, 3 g Sugar, 2 g Fib, 6 g Prot, 50 mg Calc.

FYI

Although this soup is usually served as a starter, you can make it a main course by adding an additional 1⅓ cups diced tofu and doubling the number of mushrooms. The per-serving *PointsPlus* value will increase by *2.*

Japanese Classics

FILET STEAKS WITH SESAME-WASABI BUTTER AND WATERCRESS

SERVES 4 • READY IN 20 MIN OR LESS

1   tablespoon light stick butter, at room temperature

1   teaspoon wasabi paste

3   teaspoons toasted sesame seeds

¼   teaspoon + 1 pinch salt

⅛   teaspoon + 1 pinch black pepper

▲ 4   (¼-pound) lean filet mignon steaks, trimmed

▲ 2   bunches watercress, tough stems discarded

▲ 2   scallions, thinly sliced

❶ Combine butter, wasabi paste, 2 teaspoons of sesame seeds, pinch of salt, and pinch of pepper in small bowl and mash with back of spoon until smooth. Refrigerate until ready to use.

❷ Sprinkle steaks with remaining ¼ teaspoon salt and ⅛ teaspoon pepper. Spray large nonstick skillet with nonstick spray and set over medium-high heat. Add steaks and cook, turning once, until instant-read thermometer inserted into center of steak registers 145°F for medium, about 5 minutes. Transfer steaks to platter.

❸ Add watercress and remaining 1 teaspoon sesame seeds to skillet; cook, stirring constantly, until watercress is wilted, about 2 minutes. Divide watercress among 4 plates, top with steaks, and top each steak with one quarter of butter mixture. Sprinkle with scallions and serve.

PER SERVING (1 steak, ½ cup watercress, and 1½ teaspoons wasabi butter): 215 Cal, 10 g Total Fat, 4 g Sat Fat, 0 g Trans Fat, 71 mg Chol, 312 mg Sod, 3 g Carb, 0 g Sugar, 1 g Fib, 27 g Prot, 130 mg Calc.

FILET STEAKS WITH
SESAME-WASABI BUTTER
AND WATERCRESS

NEGAMAKI-STYLE BEEF AND GREEN BEAN ROLLS

SERVES 4 • READY IN 20 MIN OR LESS

- ▲ **48 green beans (10 ounces), trimmed**
- **2 tablespoons low-fat mayonnaise**
- **½ teaspoon wasabi paste**
- **Pinch salt**
- **Pinch black pepper**
- ▲ **12 slices (¾ pound) lean sirloin roast beef**
- **½ teaspoon black sesame seeds**

1 Bring large saucepan of salted water to boil. Add green beans and cook until bright green and crisp-tender, about 5 minutes. Drain in colander under cold running water until cooled. Pat dry.

2 Meanwhile, combine mayonnaise, wasabi paste, salt, and pepper in small bowl.

3 Fold tops and bottoms of each slice of beef toward center, making even-length strips each about 2½ inches wide. Place 4 green beans on one end of each strip and roll beef around beans. Divide rolls among 4 plates, sprinkle with sesame seeds, and top with dollop of wasabi sauce.

PER SERVING (3 rolls and 1½ teaspoons wasabi sauce): 194 Cal, 6 g Total Fat, 2 g Sat Fat, 0 g Trans Fat, 49 mg Chol, 173 mg Sod, 7 g Carb, 2 g Sugar, 2 g Fib, 27 g Prot, 45 mg Calc.

5 PointsPlus value

FYI

For a perfect warm weather entrée, serve these savory rolls with chilled whole wheat noodles (a 1-cup cooked serving has a *PointsPlus* value of *4*). Sprinkle the noodles with a little soy sauce and top with grated carrot if you wish.

PORK CHOPS TONKATSU

SERVES 4

¼ cup all-purpose flour

▲ 2 large egg whites, lightly beaten

1¼ cups whole wheat panko
(Japanese bread crumbs)

▲ 4 (¼-pound) lean boneless center-cut
loin pork chops, trimmed

¼ teaspoon salt

¼ teaspoon ground sansho (Szechuan)
pepper or black pepper

¼ cup bottled tonkatsu sauce

❶ Place flour on plate, egg whites in wide shallow bowl, and panko on another plate.

❷ Sprinkle 2 pork chops with ⅛ teaspoon salt and ⅛ teaspoon sansho pepper; dip into flour, egg, and bread crumbs, turning to coat. Spray large nonstick skillet with nonstick spray and set over medium heat. Add pork chops and cook until browned and just cooked through, about 3 minutes per side. Transfer to plate and keep warm.

❸ Sprinkle remaining 2 pork chops with remaining ⅛ teaspoon salt and remaining ⅛ teaspoon sansho pepper. Prepare and cook as above, spraying skillet again with nonstick spray. Serve chops with tonkatsu sauce.

PER SERVING (1 pork chop and 1 tablespoon sauce):
311 Cal, 7 g Total Fat, 2 g Sat Fat, 0 g Trans Fat,
66 mg Chol, 829 mg Sod, 34 g Carb, 1 g Sugar, 3 g Fib,
28 g Prot, 21 mg Calc.

Japanese Classics

WARM UDON SALAD WITH SPICY PORK AND ASPARAGUS

SERVES 4

6   ounces udon noodles

▲ 8   thin asparagus spears, cut diagonally into 1½-inch lengths

1   teaspoon canola oil

▲ ¾   pound pork tenderloin, trimmed and cut into ¼ x 3-inch strips

¼   teaspoon togarashi pepper or cayenne, or to taste

2   tablespoons mirin or other sweet white wine

2   tablespoons reduced-sodium soy sauce

½   teaspoon finely grated peeled fresh ginger

¾   cup cilantro leaves

1   small avocado, cut into ½-inch cubes

❶ Cook noodles according to package directions, omitting salt and adding asparagus during last 4 minutes of cooking. Drain.

❷ Meanwhile, heat oil in large nonstick skillet or wok over medium-high heat until very hot. Add pork and togarashi and stir-fry just until pork is no longer pink, about 2 minutes. Add noodles and asparagus, mirin, soy sauce, and ginger; stir-fry until heated through, about 2 minutes. Stir in cilantro, divide among 4 bowls, and garnish noodles evenly with avocado.

PER SERVING (1⅔ cups): 367 Cal, 12 g Total Fat, 2 g Sat Fat, 0 g Trans Fat, 47 mg Chol, 297 mg Sod, 38 g Carb, 4 g Sugar, 7 g Fib, 25 g Prot, 31 mg Calc.

FYI

For more vegetable goodness, add 2 grated carrots along with the noodles and asparagus in Step 2.

Japanese Classics

CHICKEN AND VEGETABLE YAKITORI

SERVES 4

2   tablespoon reduced-sodium soy sauce

1   garlic clove, finely chopped

½   teaspoon finely grated lemon zest

⅛   teaspoon cayenne

▲ 4   (¼-pound) thin-sliced skinless chicken cutlets, each split lengthwise

▲ 32   (1-inch) squares orange or red bell pepper (about 1½ peppers)

▲ 32   (½-inch-thick) rounds small zucchini (about 3 zucchini)

▲ 32   grape or cherry tomatoes

❶ Soak 16 (12-inch) bamboo skewers in water to cover for 20 minutes. Combine soy sauce, garlic, lemon zest, and cayenne in medium bowl. Add chicken and marinate, turning frequently, 10 minutes.

❷ Preheat broiler. Cover broiler pan with aluminum foil. Thread chicken onto 8 skewers. Discard excess marinade. Thread bell pepper, zucchini, and tomatoes alternately onto remaining 8 skewers, leaving about ¼-inch space between each piece.

❸ Arrange chicken and vegetable skewers on broiler pan and spray with nonstick spray. Broil 5 inches from heat, turning once, until chicken is cooked through, about 4 minutes, and vegetables are softened, about 10 minutes.

PER SERVING (2 chicken skewers and 2 vegetable skewers): 181 Cal, 3 g Total Fat, 1 g Sat Fat, 0 g Trans Fat, 63 mg Chol, 339 mg Sod, 12 g Carb, 7 g Sugar, 4 g Fib, 26 g Prot, 44 mg Calc.

FYI

Soaking bamboo skewers in water before using keeps them from burning during cooking.

HEARTY CHICKEN AND SOBA NOODLE SOUP

SERVES 4

4 ounces soba noodles

▲ 6 asparagus spears, cut diagonally into 1½-inch lengths

▲ 4 cups reduced-sodium chicken broth

▲ 1 cup packaged coleslaw mix

▲ 6 shiitake mushrooms, stems discarded and caps thinly sliced

1 teaspoon reduced-sodium soy sauce

⅛ teaspoon ground sansho (Szechuan) pepper or black pepper

▲ ½ pound skinless boneless chicken breasts, thinly sliced

▲ ½ cup cherry tomatoes, halved

▲ 2 scallions, thinly sliced

❶ Cook soba noodles according to package directions, omitting salt; add asparagus during last 4 minutes of cooking. Drain in colander and rinse under cold running water until cooled. Drain again.

❷ Meanwhile, bring broth to boil over medium-high heat in large saucepan. Add coleslaw mix, mushrooms, soy sauce, and sansho pepper and simmer, uncovered, until mushrooms soften, about 3 minutes. Stir in chicken and soba and asparagus; cook, stirring occasionally, just until chicken is cooked through, 4–5 minutes. Remove saucepan from heat and add cherry tomatoes. Ladle into bowls and garnish with scallions.

PER SERVING (2 cups): 226 Cal, 3 g Total Fat, 1 g Sat Fat, 0 g Trans Fat, 31 mg Chol, 375 mg Sod, 32 g Carb, 3 g Sugar, 2 g Fib, 22 g Prot, 48 mg Calc.

6 PointsPlus® value

TUNA SASHIMI WITH DAIKON SALAD AND BROWN RICE

SERVES 4 • READY IN 20 MIN OR LESS

▲ 1 (3½-ounce) bag quick-cooking brown rice

¼ teaspoon salt

▲ 1 small (14-ounce) daikon radish, peeled and cut into ½-inch-thick strips

▲ 2 scallions, thinly sliced

2 tablespoons fresh lime juice

2 tablespoons reduced-sodium soy sauce

¼ teaspoon wasabi paste

▲ 1 pound fresh sushi-quality tuna, cut into long thin strips

4 teaspoons crumbled toasted nori or nori crinkles

❶ Cook brown rice according to package directions, using ⅛ teaspoon salt. Divide rice among 4 small bowls.

❷ Meanwhile, combine daikon, scallions, 1 tablespoon lime juice, and remaining ⅛ teaspoon salt in medium bowl and toss. Divide salad mixture among 4 plates.

❸ Combine soy sauce, wasabi paste, and remaining 1 tablespoon lime juice in small bowl. Divide soy mixture among 4 very small bowls and place 1 bowl on each plate to use as dipping sauce. Divide tuna among plates, sprinkle with nori, and serve immediately with rice.

PER SERVING (½ cup rice, ½ cup daikon salad, ⅔ cup tuna, and 1 tablespoon sauce): 290 Cal, 5 g Total Fat, 0 g Sat Fat, 0 g Trans Fat, 51 mg Chol, 579 mg Sod, 28 g Carb, 0 g Sugar, 1 g Fib, 35 g Prot, 51 mg Calc.

7 PointsPlus® value

FYI

It's important to use only impeccably fresh tuna for this dish: Visit a good fish market and ask for sushi-quality tuna and use it the same day you buy it. Nori is a seaweed product that comes in many forms, from large pressed sheets (commonly used for wrapping sushi) to small toasted crinkles used for garnish. You can toast large pieces of nori by holding them with tongs a few inches above an open flame just until fragrant, 2 to 3 seconds.

HALIBUT TERIYAKI WITH SESAME SNOW PEAS

SERVES 4 • READY IN 20 MIN OR LESS

3 tablespoons reduced-sodium soy sauce

1½ tablespoons packed brown sugar

1 clove garlic, quartered

½ teaspoon finely chopped peeled fresh ginger

¼ teaspoon Asian (dark) sesame oil

▲ 4 (6-ounce) halibut steaks

▲ 2 cups snow peas, trimmed

1 teaspoon toasted sesame seeds

Pinch salt

❶ Combine soy sauce, brown sugar, garlic, and ginger in small saucepan and bring to boil over medium-high heat, stirring constantly. Boil until slightly thickened, about 2 minutes. Pour through fine strainer set over small bowl; discard solids. Stir in sesame oil.

❷ Preheat broiler; cover broiler pan with aluminum foil. Brush both sides of fish with sauce. Arrange fish on pan and broil 5 inches from heat, brushing every 2 minutes with sauce, until fish is just opaque throughout, about 6 minutes.

❸ Meanwhile, bring medium saucepan of water to boil. Add snow peas and cook until crisp-tender, about 1 minute. Drain in colander, transfer to bowl, and toss with sesame seeds and salt. Serve with fish.

PER SERVING (1 halibut steak without skin and ½ cup snow peas): 235 Cal, 5 g Total Fat, 1 g Sat Fat, 0 g Trans Fat, 54 mg Chol, 532 mg Sod, 9 g Carb, 7 g Sugar, 1 g Fib, 37 g Prot, 103 mg Calc.

OURS vs. THEIRS

It's easy to love the bright flavors and elegant presentations of Japanese food, and this chapter makes it easier and healthier than ever to cook it at home. Here's how some of our delicious recipes compare with similar dishes you might find at a neighborhood restaurant.

YOUR CHOICE	OURS	THEIRS	WITH YOUR SAVINGS TRY
JAPANESE STEAK	A serving of our Filet Steaks with Sesame-Wasabi Butter and Watercress, p. 134: **5 *PointsPlus*** value	Two slices (4 ounces) restaurant-style beef teriyaki: **7 *PointsPlus*** value	¾ cup steamed edamame (in the pod): **2 *PointsPlus*** value
SOBA	A serving of our Hearty Chicken and Soba Noodle Soup, p. 142: **6 *PointsPlus*** value	1 cup cooked soba noodles with restaurant-style sauce: **12 *PointsPlus*** value	A serving of our Green Salad with Ginger-Carrot Vinaigrette, p. 132, and a 4-ounce California roll: **6 *PointsPlus*** value total
SHRIMP	A serving of our Sake-Grilled Jumbo Shrimp, p. 147: **3 *PointsPlus*** value	4-piece serving of tempura fried jumbo shrimp: **13 *PointsPlus*** value	1 cup plain cooked ramen noodles and ½ cup sake: **10 *PointsPlus*** value total
TOFU	A serving of our Sesame Tofu and Edamame Stir-Fry, p. 148: **4 *PointsPlus*** value	One piece of fried restaurant-style agadashi tofu (1½ x 2 inches): **7 *PointsPlus*** value	⅔ cup cooked brown rice: **3 *PointsPlus*** value

SAKE-GRILLED JUMBO SHRIMP

SAKE-GRILLED JUMBO SHRIMP

SERVES 4 • READY IN 20 MIN OR LESS

1½ tablespoons sake

1 tablespoon mirin or other sweet white wine

⅛ teaspoon togarashi pepper or cayenne

▲ 1½ pounds (about 24) jumbo shrimp, shelled and deveined

▲ 20 (2-inch) scallion lengths, white and light green parts only (1–2 bunches)

¼ teaspoon coarse sea salt

1 large lemon, cut into 8 wedges

❶ Combine sake, mirin, and togarashi in medium bowl. Add shrimp and marinate, turning frequently, for 15 minutes.

❷ Meanwhile, preheat broiler; cover broiler pan with aluminum foil.

❸ Remove shrimp from marinade, reserving any marinade in bowl. Thread shrimp and scallions alternately onto 4 (12-inch) metal skewers. Arrange skewers on broiler pan; brush shrimp with remaining marinade and sprinkle with ⅛ teaspoon of salt. Broil 5 inches from heat for 2 minutes. Turn skewers, sprinkle shrimp with remaining ⅛ teaspoon salt, and broil until shrimp are just opaque in middle, 2–3 minutes longer. Serve with lemon wedges.

PER SERVING (6 shrimp and 5 pieces scallion): 151 Cal, 1 g Total Fat, 0 g Sat Fat, 0 g Trans Fat, 252 mg Chol, 389 mg Sod, 3 g Carb, 2 g Sugar, 1 g Fib, 28 g Prot, 67 mg Calc.

FYI

If you like, serve the shrimp alongside a salad of butter lettuce, cucumber slices, and tomatoes tossed with soy sauce and lemon juice.

SESAME TOFU AND EDAMAME STIR-FRY

SERVES 4

2 teaspoons canola oil

▲ 1 small red onion, thinly sliced

⅛ teaspoon togarashi pepper or cayenne

▲ 1 cup frozen shelled edamame

▲ ¼ cup reduced-sodium chicken broth

1 tablespoon reduced-sodium soy sauce

▲ ½ pound extra-firm tofu, cut into ½-inch cubes

▲ 1 small red bell pepper, diced

1 tablespoon toasted sesame seeds

1 teaspoon Asian (dark) sesame oil

¼ cup snipped fresh chives or thinly sliced scallion greens

❶ Heat oil in large nonstick skillet or wok until very hot. Add onion and togarashi and stir-fry until onion is softened, about 2 minutes. Add edamame, broth, and soy sauce; stir-fry until edamame are tender, about 4 minutes. Add tofu, bell pepper, and sesame seeds and stir-fry until tofu is heated through, about 3 minutes.

❷ Remove skillet from heat and stir in sesame oil. Divide among 4 plates or bowls and sprinkle with chives.

PER SERVING (1 cup): 168 Cal, 11 g Total Fat, 1 g Sat Fat, 0 g Trans Fat, 0 mg Chol, 141 mg Sod, 8 g Carb, 2 g Sugar, 3 g Fib, 10 g Prot, 140 mg Calc.

FYI

Serve this flavorful Japanese stir-fry with either rice or noodles. A ⅔-cup serving of cooked brown rice will increase the per-serving *PointsPlus* value by *3;* 1 cup of cooked soba noodles per serving will also increase the *PointsPlus* value by *3.*

GRILLED MISO-FLAVORED EGGPLANTS WITH ADZUKI BEAN SALAD

SERVES 4

4 teaspoons white miso

2 teaspoons canola oil

2 teaspoons water

▲ 4 Japanese eggplants (each about 7 inches long)

▲ 1 (15-ounce) can no-salt-added adzuki beans, rinsed and drained

▲ 1 medium Kirby cucumber, cut into ¼-inch cubes

▲ 3 scallions, thinly sliced

2 tablespoons seasoned rice vinegar

½ teaspoon finely grated peeled fresh ginger

Pinch salt

❶ Spray grill pan or grill rack with nonstick spray; set pan over medium-high heat or preheat grill to medium high.

❷ Combine miso, oil, and water in small bowl. Halve eggplants lengthwise. With sharp knife, score flesh-side of each half, first cutting in one direction, then in opposite direction, cutting deeply but not through to skin. (Scoring eggplants will help them cook evenly.) Grill eggplants, turning frequently, until softened, about 10 minutes. Brush flesh with miso mixture and grill flesh-side up about 2 minutes longer.

❸ Meanwhile, stir together beans, cucumber, scallions, vinegar, ginger, and salt in medium bowl. Divide eggplants and bean salad among 4 plates; serve warm or at room temperature.

PER SERVING (2 eggplant halves and ½ cup bean salad): 217 Cal, 3 g Total Fat, 0 g Sat Fat, 0 g Trans Fat, 0 mg Chol, 376 mg Sod, 40 g Carb, 8 g Sugar, 13 g Fib, 11 g Prot, 45 mg Calc.

Japanese Classics

BROWN RICE GOMASIO WITH SHIITAKES AND TEMPEH

SERVES 4 • READY IN 20 MIN OR LESS

▲ 1 (3½-ounce) bag quick-cooking brown rice

2 teaspoons toasted sesame seeds

½ teaspoon coarse sea salt

2 teaspoons canola oil

6 ounces tempeh, cut into ½-inch cubes

▲ ¼ pound shiitake mushrooms, stems discarded, caps thinly sliced

▲ 4 baby carrots, cut lengthwise into matchstick strips

1 tablespoon mirin

1 teaspoon reduced-sodium soy sauce

❶ Cook brown rice according to package directions, omitting salt.

❷ Meanwhile, crush sesame seeds and salt together in mortar and pestle or on cutting board with back of small heavy pan until coarsely ground.

❸ Heat oil in large nonstick skillet over medium-high heat. Add tempeh, mushrooms, carrots, mirin, and soy sauce; cook, stirring frequently, until vegetables and tempeh are browned, about 4 minutes. Add rice and cook, stirring frequently, until vegetables are tender, about 4 minutes. Divide among 4 bowls and top with sesame seed mixture.

PER SERVING (1 cup): 167 Cal, 8 g Total Fat, 1 g Sat Fat, 0 g Trans Fat, 0 mg Chol, 252 mg Sod, 16 g Carb, 3 g Sugar, 1 g Fib, 9 g Prot, 59 mg Calc.

FYI

Gomasio, a mixture of salt and sesame seeds, is a simple and wonderful Japanese seasoning that's usually added as a garnish after cooking. It's available in Asian markets, but it's easy and inexpensive to make your own.

SCALLION EGGS WITH VEGETABLES AND TOFU

SERVES 4 • READY IN 20 MIN OR LESS

2 teaspoons canola oil

▲ ¼ pound shiitake mushrooms, tough stems discarded, caps thinly sliced

▲ 1 small zucchini, diced

▲ 4 scallions, thinly sliced

1 tablespoon reduced-sodium soy sauce

▲ 6 large egg whites

2 tablespoons chopped fresh basil

1 teaspoon chili-garlic sauce

▲ ½ (14-ounce) package firm tofu, drained and cut into ½-inch cubes

❶ Heat oil in medium nonstick skillet over medium-high heat. Add mushrooms, zucchini, scallions, and soy sauce. Cook, stirring occasionally, until vegetables soften, about 3 minutes.

❷ Meanwhile, whisk together egg whites, basil, and chili-garlic sauce in medium bowl until frothy. Add egg mixture and tofu to skillet. Reduce heat to medium and cook, stirring gently once or twice, until eggs are set, about 3 minutes. Cut into 4 wedges.

PER SERVING (1 wedge): 117 Cal, 5 g Total Fat, 1 g Sat Fat, 0 g Trans Fat, 0 mg Chol, 239 mg Sod, 8 g Carb, 3 g Sugar, 2 g Fib, 11 g Prot, 117 mg Calc.

CHAPTER 7

Chinese Favorites

Appetizers

PORK AND MUSHROOM MU SHU ROLLS

HOT-AND-SOUR SOUP WITH SMOKED TOFU

Main Courses

FLANK STEAK STIR-FRY WITH GINGER AND SCALLIONS

MA PO TOFU WITH GROUND BEEF

CHILI-GARLIC PORK WITH BOK CHOY

SPICY SZECHUAN ORANGE CHICKEN

SESAME LO MEIN WITH CHICKEN AND VEGETABLES

FIVE-SPICE DUCK BREAST WITH STEAMED BROCCOLI

KUNG PAO TURKEY WITH CASHEWS

SWEET-AND-SOUR JUMBO SHRIMP WITH PINEAPPLE

WHOLE STEAMED BASS WITH GINGER AND GARLIC

GENERAL TSO'S SCALLOPS

CURRIED SINGAPORE NOODLES WITH LOBSTER

CLAMS WITH BLACK BEAN SAUCE AND FRESH CHILE

STEAMED JADE VEGETABLES WITH TOFU

Chinese Pantry Partners

KEEP THESE STAPLES ON HAND TO QUICKLY GET HEALTHFUL MEALS ON THE TABLE.

Black Bean Sauce This ready-to-use sauce is made from fermented black beans. It's intensely flavorful and quite salty, so use it sparingly.

Chili-Garlic Sauce A thick, paste-like condiment made from hot peppers, garlic, and salt. It's excellent for quickly adding heat and flavor to dishes. It can also be used as a table condiment so that spice-loving diners can add more to their food if they wish.

Chinese Rice Wine Also known as Shaoxing wine, this amber wine is usually aged at least 10 years. It has a deep, rich flavor similar to dry sherry. Both sherry and Japanese sake are good substitutes; those who prefer to cook without alcohol can use apple juice instead.

Hoisin Sauce Sweet and tangy hoisin sauce is made from a mixture of soy beans, vinegar, sugar, salt, and chiles. It's extremely versatile: use it for everything from marinating meats to glazing grilled foods to imparting flavor to stir-fries.

Oyster Sauce This rich dark condiment is made from a combination of oyster extract and soy sauce and brings deep, smoky flavor to dishes. A version made with mushrooms instead of oysters is commonly available if you prefer not to consume shellfish, or you can substitute hoisin sauce.

Peanut Oil Preferred throughout China, this cooking oil heats to very high temperatures without burning, making it popular for stir-frying. Canola or vegetable oils are good substitutes.

Quick-Cooking or Instant Brown Rice ▲ The parboiled grains of this rice product will cook up in about 10 minutes, making it a very convenient way to get this nutritious brown rice on the table quickly.

Rice Vermicelli These very thin, thread-like noodles made from rice powder require just a quick soak in warm or boiling water to be ready to eat.

Sesame Oil Rich, aromatic sesame oil adds a distinctive nutty flavor to many Chinese dishes. Asian (dark) sesame oil and toasted sesame oils are usually "unrefined" and not recommended for high-heat cooking like stir-frying. Sesame oils labeled "refined" are suitable for stir-frying.

Chinese Favorites

PORK AND MUSHROOM MU SHU ROLLS

SERVES 8 AS AN APPETIZER

▲ ¾ pound lean pork loin, trimmed and cut into thin strips

1 tablespoon seasoned rice vinegar

1 tablespoon cornstarch

3 teaspoons reduced-sodium soy sauce

¼ cup hoisin sauce

3 teaspoons canola oil

▲ 2 (4-ounce) packages mixed sliced mushrooms

▲ 4 cups shredded Napa cabbage

▲ 2 carrots, shredded

1 tablespoon finely grated peeled fresh ginger

▲ 4 scallions, thinly sliced

8 packaged crêpes, warmed according to package directions

1 Combine pork, vinegar, cornstarch, and 2 teaspoons soy sauce in medium bowl and toss to coat. Combine remaining 1 teaspoon soy sauce and hoisin sauce in small bowl.

2 Heat 2 teaspoons oil in wok or large nonstick skillet over medium-high heat until very hot. Add pork and stir-fry until cooked through, about 4 minutes; transfer to plate. Return skillet to heat and add remaining 1 teaspoon oil. Add mushrooms and cook, stirring occasionally, until browned, about 6 minutes. Add cabbage, carrots, and ginger and cook, stirring often, until cabbage is crisp-tender, 3–4 minutes. Stir in pork, scallions, and hoisin mixture and cook until heated thoroughly through, about 2 minutes.

3 Place 1 crêpe on work surface and top with ½ cup pork mixture. Fold bottom of crêpe over filling, fold in sides, and roll crêpe up. Repeat with remaining crêpes and filling.

PER SERVING (1 filled crêpe): 155 Cal, 6 g Total Fat, 1 g Sat Fat, 0 g Trans Fat, 30 mg Chol, 303 mg Sod, 14 g Carb, 6 g Sugar, 2 g Fib, 12 g Prot, 38 mg Calc.

4 PointsPlus® value

PORK AND MUSHROOM MU SHU ROLLS,
AND HOT-AND-SOUR SOUP WITH
SMOKED TOFU, PAGE 158

HOT-AND-SOUR SOUP WITH SMOKED TOFU

SERVES 4 AS AN APPETIZER

▲ 12 dried wood-ear mushrooms

3 tablespoons seasoned rice vinegar

2 teaspoons reduced-sodium soy sauce

2 teaspoons hot pepper sauce

▲ 4 cups reduced-sodium vegetable broth

▲ 1 (8-ounce) package smoked tofu, cut into ½-inch cubes

▲ 1 (15-ounce) can baby corn, drained

▲ 1 (8-ounce) can sliced bamboo shoots, drained

▲ 1 cup thinly sliced asparagus tips

2 tablespoons cornstarch

2 tablespoons + 2 teaspoons cold water

▲ 1 large egg white

▲ 2 scallions, thinly sliced

1 Place mushrooms in large bowl and pour in hot water to cover; let stand 15 minutes. Combine vinegar, soy sauce, and hot pepper sauce in separate bowl.

2 Meanwhile, bring broth to boil in large saucepan over medium-high heat. Stir in vinegar mixture, tofu, baby corn, and bamboo shoots. Return to boil; reduce heat to medium and simmer, uncovered, 10 minutes.

3 Drain mushrooms and add to saucepan along with asparagus. Increase heat to medium-high and return to boil. Stir cornstarch and 2 tablespoons cold water together in small bowl. Whisk cornstarch mixture into soup and cook until thickened, about 1 minute. Remove from heat. Beat egg white with remaining 2 teaspoons water; drizzle over soup, stirring gently to make ribbons of egg white. Stir in scallions.

PER SERVING (1¾ cups): 265 Cal, 4 g Total Fat, 0 g Sat Fat, 0 g Trans Fat, 0 mg Chol, 493 mg Sod, 36 g Carb, 5 g Sugar, 14 g Fib, 12 g Prot, 170 mg Calc.

FYI

Dried wood-ear mushrooms (sometimes called dried black fungus or dried tree fungus) can be found in Asian markets.

FLANK STEAK STIR-FRY WITH GINGER AND SCALLIONS

SERVES 4 • READY IN 20 MIN OR LESS

▲ ¾ **cup quick-cooking brown rice**

▲ ¾ **pound flank steak, trimmed and thinly sliced**

1 **teaspoon cornstarch**

4 **teaspoons reduced-sodium soy sauce**

3 **tablespoons hoisin sauce**

1 **tablespoon peanut oil**

1 **tablespoon finely grated peeled fresh ginger**

▲ ½ **large red bell pepper, cut into thin strips**

▲ ½ **large green bell pepper, cut into thin strips**

▲ 5 **scallions, cut into 1-inch pieces**

1 **teaspoon toasted sesame seeds**

❶ Cook rice according to package directions, omitting salt and fat.

❷ Combine steak, cornstarch, and 2 teaspoons soy sauce in medium bowl and toss to coat. Combine remaining 2 teaspoons soy sauce with hoisin in small bowl.

❸ Heat oil in wok or large nonstick skillet over medium-high heat until very hot. Add beef and cook, stirring occasionally, just until lightly browned, about 45 seconds. Add ginger and cook 30 seconds. Stir in bell peppers and cook, stirring often, until crisp-tender, about 2 minutes. Add hoisin mixture and cook, stirring, 30 seconds. Remove from heat; stir in scallions and sprinkle with sesame seeds. Divide beef mixture and rice among 4 plates.

PER SERVING (¾ cup beef mixture and ½ cup rice): 260 Cal, 10 g Total Fat, 3 g Sat Fat, 0 g Trans Fat, 32 mg Chol, 368 mg Sod, 23 g Carb, 5 g Sugar, 2 g Fib, 21 g Prot, 43 mg Calc.

Chinese Favorites

MA PO TOFU WITH GROUND BEEF

SERVES 4 • READY IN 20 MIN OR LESS

- ▲ 1 (14-ounce) package lite firm tofu
- ▲ ¾ cup quick-cooking brown rice
- ▲ ½ cup reduced-sodium chicken broth
- 2 tablespoons oyster sauce
- 1 tablespoon reduced-sodium soy sauce
- 1 tablespoon cornstarch
- ▲ 6 ounces ground lean beef (7% fat or less)
- 4 garlic cloves, minced
- 1 tablespoon finely grated peeled fresh ginger
- ▲ 2 scallions, chopped

① Drain tofu; place entire block on plate lined with paper towels. Set another plate on top to weight it. Let stand 10 minutes to remove excess liquid. Pour off liquid and cut tofu into ¹/₂-inch cubes.

② Meanwhile, cook rice according to package directions, omitting salt and fat. Combine broth, oyster sauce, soy sauce, and cornstarch in small bowl.

③ Heat large nonstick skillet over medium-high heat. Add beef and cook, breaking up chunks with side of wooden spoon, until no longer pink, about 3 minutes. Add garlic and ginger and stir-fry 1 minute. Add tofu and cook just until lightly browned, 3–4 minutes. Stir in broth mixture; bring to boil and cook until thickened, about 1 minute. Remove from heat and stir in scallions. Serve over rice.

PER SERVING (¾ cup tofu mixture and ½ cup rice):
271 Cal, 5 g Total Fat, 1 g Sat Fat, 0 g Trans Fat, 26 mg Chol, 414 mg Sod, 35 g Carb, 0 g Sugar, 3 g Fib, 21 g Prot, 213 mg Calc.

CHILI-GARLIC PORK WITH BOK CHOY

SERVES 4 • READY IN 20 MIN OR LESS

▲ 1 **pound lean pork tenderloin, trimmed and cut into ½-inch thick slices**

3 **teaspoons reduced-sodium soy sauce**

3 **teaspoons oyster sauce**

2 **teaspoons cornstarch**

▲ ⅓ **cup reduced-sodium chicken broth**

1 **teaspoon chili-garlic sauce**

2 **teaspoons canola oil**

3 **garlic cloves, minced**

1 **tablespoon finely grated peeled fresh ginger**

▲ 1 **pound baby bok choy (about 8), each halved lengthwise**

▲ 1 **large red bell pepper, cut into ½-inch pieces**

❶ Combine pork, 1 teaspoon soy sauce, 1 teaspoon oyster sauce, and 1 teaspoon cornstarch in medium bowl and toss to coat. Combine broth, chili-garlic sauce, remaining 2 teaspoons soy sauce, 2 teaspoons oyster sauce, and 1 teaspoon cornstarch in small bowl.

❷ Heat 1 teaspoon oil in wok or large nonstick skillet over medium-high heat until very hot. Add pork and cook, stirring occasionally, until it is lightly browned and just cooked through, 3–4 minutes. Transfer to plate.

❸ Return skillet to heat and add remaining 1 teaspoon oil. Stir in garlic and ginger. Add bok choy and bell pepper; stir-fry until bok choy is bright green, about 2 minutes. Stir in pork, then add broth mixture and cook until sauce thickens and pork is heated through, about 2 minutes.

PER SERVING (1¾ cups): 186 Cal, 6 g Total Fat, 1 g Sat Fat, 0 g Trans Fat, 62 mg Chol, 353 mg Sod, 8 g Carb, 3 g Sugar, 2 g Fib, 25 g Prot, 15 mg Calc.

FYI

This is an excellent dish to serve with noodles. A 1-cup serving of cooked soba noodles has a per-serving *PointsPlus* value of *3.*

SPICY SZECHUAN ORANGE CHICKEN

SERVES 4

- ▲ ¾ cup quick-cooking brown rice
- ▲ 1 pound boneless skinless chicken breast, cut into thin strips
- 2 teaspoons finely grated orange zest
- 1 tablespoon + 2 teaspoons cornstarch
- 2 tablespoons reduced-sodium soy sauce
- ½ cup orange juice
- ▲ ⅓ cup reduced-sodium chicken broth
- 2 teaspoons honey
- 1 teaspoon Asian (dark) sesame oil
- ¼ teaspoon red pepper flakes, or to taste
- 2 teaspoons canola oil
- 1 tablespoon finely grated peeled fresh ginger
- 2 garlic cloves, sliced
- ▲ ½ bunch broccoli, cut into florets (3 cups)
- ▲ 2 carrots, thinly sliced on diagonal

1 Cook rice according to package directions, omitting salt and fat.

2 Meanwhile, combine chicken, orange zest, 1 tablespoon cornstarch, and 1 tablespoon soy sauce in large bowl and toss to coat. Combine orange juice, broth, honey, sesame oil, pepper flakes, remaining 2 teaspoons cornstarch, and remaining 1 tablespoon soy sauce in small bowl.

3 Heat 1 teaspoon canola oil in wok or large nonstick skillet over medium-high heat until very hot. Add chicken and stir-fry until lightly browned, about 3 minutes; transfer to plate. Return skillet to heat and add remaining 1 teaspoon canola oil. Add ginger and garlic; stir-fry until fragrant, about 15 seconds. Stir in broccoli and carrots and stir-fry until broccoli is bright green, about 2 minutes. Pour in orange juice mixture; bring to boil and cook until thickened, about 1 minute. Add chicken and cook until heated through, about 1 minute. Divide chicken mixture and rice among 4 plates.

PER SERVING (1 cup chicken mixture and ½ cup rice): 282 Cal, 7 g Total Fat, 1 g Sat Fat, 0 g Trans Fat, 63 mg Chol, 304 mg Sod, 28 g Carb, 6 g Sugar, 4 g Fib, 28 g Prot, 72 mg Calc.

7 PointsPlus® value

SESAME LO MEIN WITH CHICKEN AND VEGETABLES

SERVES 6

6   ounces lo mein noodles

1   teaspoon Asian (dark) sesame oil

▲ ¼   cup reduced-sodium chicken broth

3   tablespoons reduced-sodium soy sauce

3   tablespoons Chinese rice wine or dry sherry

▲ ¾   pound boneless skinless chicken breast, cut into ¾-inch pieces

2   teaspoons canola oil

▲ ¼   pound shiitake mushrooms, stems discarded, caps thinly sliced

2   garlic cloves, minced

▲ 4   cups shredded Napa cabbage

▲ ¼   pound snow peas

▲ 4   scallions, chopped

1   teaspoon toasted sesame seeds

❶ Cook noodles according to package directions, omitting salt. Drain in colander under cold water. Drain again. Transfer to medium bowl and toss with sesame oil. Combine broth, 2 tablespoons soy sauce, and 2 tablespoons rice wine in cup.

❷ Combine chicken pieces with remaining 1 tablespoon soy sauce in another bowl and toss. Heat 1 teaspoon canola oil in wok or large nonstick skillet over medium-high heat until very hot. Add chicken and cook, stirring occasionally, until browned, 3–4 minutes; transfer to plate.

❸ Return skillet to heat and add remaining 1 teaspoon canola oil. Add mushrooms and stir-fry until softened, 2–3 minutes. Add garlic and stir-fry 30 seconds. Add cabbage, snow peas, and remaining 1 tablespoon rice wine; stir-fry until cabbage has wilted and snow peas are bright green, 2–3 minutes. Stir in noodles, chicken, and soy sauce mixture and cook, tossing, until heated thoroughly through, about 2 minutes. Remove from heat and sprinkle with scallions and sesame seeds.

PER SERVING (1 cup): 273 Cal, 10 g Total Fat, 2 g Sat Fat, 0 g Trans Fat, 31 mg Chol, 445 mg Sod, 25 g Carb, 2 g Sugar, 4 g Fib, 19 g Prot, 48 mg Calc.

7 PointsPlus® value

Chinese Favorites

FIVE-SPICE DUCK BREAST WITH STEAMED BROCCOLI

SERVES 4 • READY IN 20 MIN OR LESS

▲ ½ large bunch broccoli, cut into florets (4 cups)

4 (6-ounce) boneless duck breast halves, skin removed and discarded

1 teaspoon Chinese five-spice powder

¼ teaspoon salt

3 teaspoons canola oil

1 small shallot, chopped

2 garlic cloves, minced

2 teaspoons finely grated peeled fresh ginger

¼ cup Chinese rice wine or dry sherry

⅓ cup no-sugar-added apricot fruit spread

1 tablespoon reduced-sodium soy sauce

❶ Steam broccoli in vegetable steamer until bright green and crisp-tender, about 4 minutes. Keep warm.

❷ Meanwhile, sprinkle duck with five-spice powder and salt. Heat 2 teaspoons oil in large nonstick skillet over medium-high heat. Add duck and cook, turning once, until browned and medium-rare, about 6 minutes. Transfer to plate and keep warm. Return skillet to heat and add remaining 1 teaspoon oil. Add shallot, garlic, and ginger; cook, stirring, until very fragrant, 30 seconds. Stir in wine and cook until nearly evaporated. Add fruit spread and soy sauce and cook, stirring, 30 seconds.

❸ Thinly slice duck and fan on 4 plates. Divide broccoli among plates; spoon sauce over duck.

PER SERVING (1 duck breast half, 2 tablespoons sauce, and 1 cup broccoli): 227 Cal, 8 g Total Fat, 2 g Sat Fat, 0 g Trans Fat, 71 mg Chol, 322 mg Sod, 22 g Carb, 12 g Sugar, 2 g Fib, 21 g Prot, 51 mg Calc.

FYI

Try this delicious duck with a side of your favorite whole grain. Quick-cooking barley can be ready in less than 20 minutes and has a *PointsPlus* value of *3* per ⅔-cup serving.

KUNG PAO TURKEY WITH CASHEWS

SERVES 4 • READY IN 20 MIN OR LESS

▲ 1 **pound boneless skinless turkey breast, cut into ¾-inch pieces**

3 **garlic cloves, minced**

1 **tablespoon finely grated peeled fresh ginger**

1 **teaspoon cornstarch**

3 **tablespoons reduced-sodium soy sauce**

3 **teaspoons seasoned rice vinegar**

1 **teaspoon Asian (dark) sesame oil**

1 **teaspoon sugar**

2 **teaspoons canola oil**

¼ **teaspoon crushed red pepper flakes**

▲ 1 **medium red bell pepper, cut into ¾-inch pieces**

▲ 1 **(8-ounce) can sliced bamboo shoots, drained**

⅓ **cup roasted unsalted cashews**

❶ Combine turkey, garlic, ginger, cornstarch, 1 tablespoon soy sauce, and 1 teaspoon vinegar in medium bowl and toss to coat. Combine remaining 2 tablespoons soy sauce, 2 teaspoons vinegar, sesame oil, and sugar in cup.

❷ Heat canola oil in wok or large nonstick skillet over medium-high heat until very hot. Add pepper flakes and cook, stirring, 15 seconds. Add turkey and stir-fry until no longer pink, about 2 minutes. Add bell pepper and bamboo shoots and stir-fry 1 minute. Add cashews and cook 30 seconds. Stir in soy sauce mixture; bring to boil and cook, stirring, until bell pepper is crisp-tender and turkey is cooked through, 1–2 minutes.

PER SERVING (1 cup): 248 Cal, 10 g Total Fat, 2 g Sat Fat, 0 g Trans Fat, 74 mg Chol, 420 mg Sod, 9 g Carb, 3 g Sugar, 1 g Fib, 31 g Prot, 27 mg Calc.

FYI

This richly flavored stir-fry is excellent paired with steamed baby bok choy.

SWEET-AND-SOUR JUMBO SHRIMP WITH PINEAPPLE

SERVES 4 • READY IN 20 MIN OR LESS

▲ ¾ cup quick-cooking brown rice

▲ 1 (8-ounce) can pineapple chunks in juice, drained (reserve juice)

  3 tablespoons rice vinegar

  3 tablespoons ketchup

  1 tablespoon reduced-sodium soy sauce

  1 tablespoon cornstarch

  2 teaspoons sugar

  3 teaspoons canola oil

▲ 1½ pounds jumbo shrimp, peeled and deveined

▲ 1 green bell pepper, cut into ½-inch pieces

▲ 1 cup shredded carrot

▲ 2 scallions, thinly sliced

❶ Cook rice according to package directions, omitting salt and fat.

❷ Meanwhile, combine reserved pineapple juice, vinegar, ketchup, soy sauce, cornstarch, and sugar in medium bowl.

❸ Heat 2 teaspoons oil in a large nonstick skillet over medium-high heat. Add shrimp and cook, turning once, until just opaque, 4–5 minutes; transfer to plate. Return skillet to heat and add remaining 1 teaspoon oil. Add bell pepper and carrot and stir-fry until crisp-tender, about 3 minutes. Add pineapple chunks and cook 1 minute. Add pineapple juice mixture and shrimp; bring to boil and cook until sauce thickens, about 1 minute. Divide shrimp and rice among 4 plates or bowls and sprinkle with scallions.

PER SERVING (1⅓ cups shrimp and ½ cup rice): 295 Cal, 5 g Total Fat, 1 g Sat Fat, 0 g Trans Fat, 252 mg Chol, 537 mg Sod, 32 g Carb, 14 g Sugar, 3 g Fib, 30 g Prot, 86 mg Calc.

Chinese Favorites

WHOLE STEAMED BASS WITH GINGER AND GARLIC

SERVES 2

▲ 1 (2-pound) head-on whole sea bass, cleaned and scaled

3 garlic cloves, minced

1 tablespoon finely grated peeled fresh ginger

1 teaspoon canola oil

Pinch red pepper flakes

2 slices peeled fresh ginger (each about the size of a quarter), cut into matchsticks

▲ 1 small carrot, cut into thin strips

▲ 3 scallions, halved crosswise and cut into thin strips

1½ tablespoons reduced-sodium soy sauce

1 tablespoon rice vinegar

2 tablespoons chopped fresh cilantro

1 Rinse fish under cold water and pat dry with paper towels. With sharp knife, make 4 parallel diagonal slashes, down to bone, on each side of fish. Combine garlic, grated ginger, oil, and pepper flakes and rub over fish and inside cavity. Combine ginger strips, carrot, and scallions in bowl. Place one third of carrot mixture on large heatproof plate. Set fish on top, place one third of mixture into cavity, and remaining one third over top of fish. Sprinkle with soy sauce and vinegar.

2 Put plate in bamboo steamer basket; set in wok or pan over boiling water. Cover tightly and steam until fish is opaque in center and flakes easily with fork, 14–16 minutes. Remove plate with fish from steamer. Garnish with cilantro.

PER SERVING (½ fish): 271 Cal, 7 g Total Fat, 1 g Sat Fat, 0 g Trans Fat, 92 mg Chol, 467 mg Sod, 7 g Carb, 2 g Sugar, 1 g Fib, 43 g Prot, 58 mg Calc.

FYI

When buying whole fish look for very clear eyes, shiny skin, and bright-red gills, all signs of freshness. We suggest a small sea bass for this recipe, but you could also substitute just about any 2-pound whole fish, including porgy, croaker, or whiting.

Chinese Favorites

GENERAL TSO'S SCALLOPS

SERVES 4 • READY IN 20 MIN OR LESS

▲ 1 **pound sea scallops**

¼ **cup Chinese rice wine or dry sherry**

4 **teaspoons oyster sauce**

4 **teaspoons cornstarch**

1 **tablespoon rice vinegar**

2 **teaspoons sugar**

1 **teaspoon chili-garlic sauce**

4 **teaspoons canola oil**

1 **tablespoon finely grated peeled fresh ginger**

▲ 2 **scallions, chopped**

▲ 3 **celery stalks, cut into ½-inch slices**

▲ 1 **large red bell pepper, cut into ¾-inch pieces**

❶ Combine scallops, 2 tablespoons rice wine, 2 teaspoons oyster sauce, and 3 teaspoons corn-starch in medium bowl; toss to coat. Combine vinegar, sugar, chili-garlic sauce, remaining 2 tablespoons rice wine, remaining 2 teaspoons oyster sauce, and remaining 1 teaspoon cornstarch in separate bowl.

❷ Heat 2 teaspoons oil in wok or large nonstick skillet over medium-high heat until very hot. Add one half of scallops and cook until browned, about 2 minutes per side; transfer to plate. Add 1 teaspoon of remaining oil to skillet and repeat with remaining scallops.

❸ Wipe out skillet with paper towel and return to heat. Add remaining 1 teaspoon oil. Add ginger and scallions and stir-fry until fragrant, about 30 seconds. Add celery and bell pepper; cook, stirring often, until starting to soften, 2–3 minutes. Add scallops and rice wine mixture; cook, stirring, until sauce thickens and scallops are cooked through, about 2 minutes.

PER SERVING (1 cup): 201 Cal, 6 g Total Fat, 0 g Sat Fat, 0 g Trans Fat, 37 mg Chol, 422 mg Sod, 13 g Carb, 4 g Sugar, 2 g Fib, 20 g Prot, 53 mg Calc.

OURS vs.THEIRS

If you crave Chinese you're not alone: Survey after survey has found it as either the first or second choice of those seeking takeout food for dinner. What's *not* to love? The high *PointsPlus* values for many restaurant favorites—that's what. Here's how some of the quick and easy recipes in this chapter compare with dishes you might find at your local Chinese joint.

YOUR CHOICE	OURS	THEIRS	WITH YOUR SAVINGS TRY
BEEF STIR-FRY	A serving of our Flank Steak Stir-Fry with Ginger and Scallions, p. 159: *7 PointsPlus* value	A 1-cup serving of restaurant-style orange-ginger beef: *15 PointsPlus* value	A serving of our Hot-and-Sour Soup with Smoked Tofu, p. 158, and 2 fig bars: *8 PointsPlus* value total
LO MEIN	A serving of our Sesame Lo Mein with Chicken and Vegetables, p. 163: *7 PointsPlus* value	A 1-cup serving of restaurant-style chicken lo mein: *9 PointsPlus* value	1 scoop (½ cup) sorbet: *2 PointsPlus* value
DUCK	A serving of our Five Spice Duck Breast with Steamed Broccoli, p. 164: *7 PointsPlus* value	A 2-ounce serving of Peking duck with skin and 3 pancakes: *11 PointsPlus* value	4 store-bought steamed vegetable dumplings: *4 PointsPlus* value
KUNG PAO	A serving of our Kung Pao Turkey with Cashews, p. 166: *6 PointsPlus* value	A 1-cup serving of restaurant-style kung pao chicken: *9 PointsPlus* value	A cup of egg drop soup and 2 fortune cookies: *3 PointsPlus* value total
BLACK BEAN SAUCE	A serving of our Clams with Black Bean Sauce and Fresh Chile, p. 174: *5 PointsPlus* value	A 1-cup serving of restaurant-style chicken with black bean sauce: *8 PointsPlus* value	1 (4-ounce) glass white wine: *3 PointsPlus* value

CURRIED SINGAPORE NOODLES WITH LOBSTER

SERVES 4 • READY IN 20 MIN OR LESS

6   ounces rice vermicelli

▲ ⅔ cup low-sodium chicken broth

2   tablespoons reduced-sodium soy sauce

1   tablespoon Chinese rice wine or
      dry sherry

½   teaspoon sugar

▲ 2   (8-ounce) thawed frozen lobster tails

1   tablespoon canola oil

3   garlic cloves, minced

1   tablespoon finely grated peeled
      fresh ginger

▲ 1   large red bell pepper, cut into thin strips

2   teaspoons curry powder

▲ 4   scallions, sliced on the diagonal

❶ Prepare noodles according to package directions. Drain in colander under cold running water. Drain again. Meanwhile, combine broth, soy sauce, wine, and sugar in small bowl.

❷ Remove lobster meat from shells and cut it into chunks. Heat oil in wok or large nonstick skillet over medium-high heat until very hot. Add lobster and cook, stirring, until just opaque, about 3 minutes. Add garlic and ginger; stir-fry 1 minute. Add bell pepper and stir-fry until softened, about 1 minute. Add curry powder and stir-fry 15 seconds. Stir in noodles and broth mixture. Cook, tossing, until liquid evaporates and noodles are hot, about 2 minutes. Remove from heat and stir in scallions.

PER SERVING (1½ cups): 333 Cal, 5 g Total Fat, 1 g Sat Fat, 0 g Trans Fat, 94 mg Chol, 578 mg Sod, 40 g Carb, 2 g Sugar, 2 g Fib, 24 g Prot, 76 mg Calc.

FYI

You'll find frozen lobster tails at fish markets and at some supermarkets. It's best to thaw them in the refrigerator overnight, although you can also place them in a zip-close plastic bag and submerge the bag in a bowl of cold water just until the tails are flexible, about 1 hour.

CURRIED SINGAPORE
NOODLES WITH LOBSTER

CLAMS WITH BLACK BEAN SAUCE AND FRESH CHILE

SERVES 4 • READY IN 20 MIN OR LESS

1   tablespoon peanut oil

▲ 1   onion, diced

3   garlic cloves, minced

▲ 1–2 small red Thai chiles, seeded and sliced

▲ 40 littleneck clams, scrubbed

▲ ½   cup reduced-sodium chicken broth

1   tablespoon black bean sauce

1   tablespoon hoisin sauce

2   tablespoons chopped fresh cilantro

❶ Heat oil in wok or large skillet over medium-high heat. Add onion, garlic, and chiles; cook, stirring, until onion softens, about 2 minutes. Add clams and cook 1 minute. Stir in broth, black bean sauce, and hoisin sauce; cover and cook until clams open, 6–8 minutes.

❷ Discard any clams that do not open. Divide clams among 4 bowls and spoon sauce from pan over each serving. Sprinkle with cilantro.

PER SERVING (10 clams and ⅓ cup sauce): 207 Cal, 6 g Total Fat, 1 g Sat Fat, 0 g Trans Fat, 64 mg Chol, 210 mg Sod, 12 g Carb, 4 g Sugar, 1 g Fib, 26 g Prot, 107 mg Calc.

FYI

We suggest you use either one or two small, fiery Thai chiles in this dish, but you could substitute red pepper flakes to taste.

STEAMED JADE VEGETABLES WITH TOFU

SERVES 4

▲ 1 (15-ounce) package firm tofu, drained

▲ ¾ cup quick-cooking brown rice

▲ 3 large lettuce or cabbage leaves

▲ ¾ bunch broccoli, cut into florets (5 cups)

▲ 2 small zucchini, split lengthwise then cut crosswise into ½-inch-thick slices

▲ ¼ pound green beans, trimmed

▲ ¼ pound snow peas

3 tablespoons reduced-sodium soy sauce

1 tablespoon rice vinegar

1 teaspoon finely grated peeled fresh ginger

3 tablespoons water

❶ Drain tofu; place entire block on plate lined with paper towels. Set another plate on top to weight it. Let stand 10 minutes to remove excess liquid. Pour off liquid and cut tofu into 1-inch pieces.

❷ Meanwhile, cook rice according to package directions, omitting salt and fat.

❸ Line large bamboo or metal steamer basket with lettuce leaves. Toss to combine broccoli, zucchini, green beans, and snow peas in large bowl. Transfer mixture to steamer and top with tofu; set in saucepan or large skillet over 1 inch of boiling water. Cover tightly and steam vegetables until bright green and crisp-tender, about 5 minutes.

❹ Combine soy sauce, vinegar, ginger, and water in small bowl. Divide rice among 4 bowls and top with vegetable mixture. Spoon 1½ tablespoons sauce over each serving.

PER SERVING (2¼ cups vegetables, ½ cup rice, and 1½ tablespoons sauce): 231 Cal, 6 g Total Fat, 1 g Sat Fat, 0 g Trans Fat, 0 mg Chol, 392 mg Sod, 31 g Carb, 5 g Sugar, 7 g Fib, 17 g Prot, 306 mg Calc.

CHAPTER 8

Thai, Vietnamese, and Korean Specialties

Appetizers

GREEN PAPAYA SALAD

SUMMER ROLLS WITH CRAB AND MANGO

Main Courses

KOREAN STEAK KEBABS WITH SPICY CILANTRO SAUCE

BEEF PHO BO SOUP

LEMONGRASS PORK SATAY WITH SPICY CUCUMBER SALAD

ROASTED BARBECUE PORK WITH FRESH KIMCHI

CHICKEN BANH MI SANDWICHES

KOREAN-STYLE SWEET-AND-SPICY CHICKEN ROLLS

CRISPY TUNA WITH APRICOT-WASABI SAUCE

THAI SALMON IN CURRY BROTH

SHRIMP AND PINEAPPLE CURRY

SAIGON SEAFOOD POT

VEGETABLE PAD THAI

Pantry Partners
KEEP THESE STAPLES ON HAND TO QUICKLY GET HEALTHFUL MEALS ON THE TABLE.

Asian Fish Sauce This pungent, salty condiment is derived from salted fermented fish. It's known as *nam pla* in Thailand and *nuoc nam* in Vietnam.

Coconut Milk Rich, naturally sweet coconut milk is a staple ingredient in many Southeast Asian soups and curries. Using light (reduced-fat) coconut milk instead of regular coconut milk will deliver good flavor and creaminess while trimming the number of fat grams in your recipes.

Lemongrass Look for fresh lemongrass in the produce section of your supermarket or in Asian specialty stores. To prepare it, peel off the green, fibrous husk of the stalks and finely chop the pale core. If you can't find lemongrass, you can substitute a mixture of equal parts of minced fresh ginger and lime zest.

Rice Paper Wrappers Called "rice paper" because of their paper-thin texture, these are the classic wrapper for summer rolls. The dried, brittle wrappers are soaked briefly in hot water until pliable.

Rice Stick Noodles Made from rice flour and water, these noodles come in a variety of widths. Thin rice stick noodles are popular in spring rolls and soups, while wider noodles are the traditional for making pad thai.

Sambal Olek A fiery blend of ground chiles, vinegar, and salt, sambal olek is used throughout Southeast Asia as both a cooking ingredient and a table condiment. You can use Sriracha or other chili sauces as a substitute.

Sriracha This Thai-style chili sauce is available in most supermarkets and is a good all-purpose hot sauce to use in Southeast Asian dishes. The most popular brand is sold in convenient squeeze bottles with a white rooster on the label.

Thai Chile Peppers ▲ A.k.a. bird chiles, these tiny, super-spicy peppers are the standard chiles for Southeast Asian cooking. If you prefer, you can substitute milder serrano or jalapeño peppers.

Thai Curry Paste Small jars of thick, pungent concentrated Thai-style curry pastes are available in most large supermarkets. Red and green varieties are the most popular.

GREEN PAPAYA SALAD

SERVES 4 AS AN APPETIZER

▲ ¼   pound slender green beans or haricots verts, trimmed and cut into 2-inch pieces

3   tablespoons lime juice

2   teaspoons Asian fish sauce

2   teaspoons honey

2   teaspoons grated peeled fresh ginger

1   teaspoon reduced-sodium soy sauce

▲ 1   jalapeño pepper, seeded and minced

1   garlic clove, minced

▲ 1   (1-pound) green papaya, peeled, halved, seeded, and cut into ½-inch chunks

▲ 1   cup cherry tomatoes, halved

¼   cup fresh cilantro leaves

1   tablespoon dry-roasted peanuts

❶ Bring large saucepan of water to boil. Add green beans; return to boil and cook until crisp-tender, about 3 minutes. Drain in colander under cold running water to cool. Drain again.

❷ Whisk together lime juice, fish sauce, honey, ginger, soy sauce, jalapeño, and garlic in large bowl. Add beans, papaya, tomatoes, and cilantro to bowl and toss to coat. Sprinkle with peanuts.

PER SERVING (1 cup): 77 Cal, 1 g Total Fat, 0 g Sat Fat, 0 g Trans Fat, 0 mg Chol, 283 mg Sod, 16 g Carb, 9 g Sugar, 3 g Fib, 2 g Prot, 39 mg Calc.

FYI

You can find firm, green unripe papayas in Asian markets or in the produce section of some health food stores. Their tang and crunch make them popular in Southeast Asian cooking, particularly in salads. Jicama is a good substitute if you can't find green papaya.

SUMMER ROLLS WITH CRAB AND MANGO

SERVES 4 AS AN APPETIZER

2½ tablespoons reduced-sodium soy sauce

1 tablespoon lime juice

2 teaspoons honey

1 teaspoon sambal olek or chili-garlic paste

½ teaspoon Asian (dark) sesame oil

8 (6-inch) round rice paper wrappers

▲ 4 large Boston lettuce leaves, each cut lengthwise in half

▲ 1 small mango, peeled, pitted, and cut lengthwise into thin strips

▲ 1 red bell pepper, cut into thin strips

▲ 2 cups bean sprouts

▲ 4 imitation crab sticks (6 ounces), each cut lengthwise in half

16 sprigs fresh cilantro

① To make dipping sauce, whisk together soy sauce, lime juice, honey, sambal olek, and sesame oil in small bowl.

② To assemble rolls, working one at a time, dip rice paper wrappers in bowl of warm water; let stand just until soft, about 30 seconds. Place on clean kitchen towel. Place 1 lettuce piece in center of each wrapper. Top lettuce with one eighth of mango, bell pepper, and bean sprouts. Top each with piece of crab stick and 2 cilantro sprigs. Fold in sides and roll up to enclose filling. Press gently to seal. Cut each roll in half on diagonal. Serve with dipping sauce.

PER SERVING (2 rolls and 1½ tablespoons sauce): 191 Cal, 2 g Total Fat, 0 g Sat Fat, 0 g Trans Fat, 9 mg Chol, 750 mg Sod, 39 g Carb, 18 g Sugar, 3 g Fib, 9 g Prot, 33 mg Calc.

KOREAN STEAK KEBABS WITH SPICY CILANTRO SAUCE

SERVES 4 • READY IN 20 MIN OR LESS

¼ cup chopped fresh cilantro

3 tablespoons reduced-sodium soy sauce

2 tablespoons mirin

1 tablespoon grated peeled fresh ginger

2 teaspoons chili-garlic sauce

1 teaspoon Asian (dark) sesame oil

▲ 1 pound lean beef tenderloin, trimmed and cut diagonally into thin strips

▲ 4 scallions, cut into 2-inch lengths

1 To make sauce, combine cilantro, soy sauce, mirin, ginger, chili-garlic sauce, and ½ teaspoon sesame oil in small bowl.

2 Spray broiler rack with nonstick spray; preheat broiler.

3 Toss beef, scallions, and remaining ½ teaspoon sesame oil in large bowl. Thread beef and scallions onto 4 metal skewers. Place skewers on broiler rack and broil 5 inches from heat, turning occasionally, until browned, 4–5 minutes for medium-rare. Serve with sauce.

PER SERVING (1 skewer with 2 tablespoons sauce): 207 Cal, 8 g Total Fat, 3 g Sat Fat, 0 g Trans Fat, 67 mg Chol, 486 mg Sod, 5 g Carb, 3 g Sugar, 1 g Fib, 25 g Prot, 29 mg Calc.

FYI

Broiled mushrooms make a tasty accompaniment to this steak. Thread 10 ounces of small cremini mushrooms onto metal skewers and broil them alongside the steak, turning them occasionally, until tender and browned.

KOREAN STEAK KEBABS WITH
SPICY CILANTRO SAUCE

BEEF PHO BO SOUP

SERVES 4

4 ounces rice stick noodles

▲ 1 pound lean flank steak, trimmed

▲ 3 cups reduced-sodium beef broth

1 cup water

▲ 6 large radishes, trimmed and thinly sliced

▲ 6 scallions, each cut diagonally into 3 pieces

1 (2-inch) piece peeled fresh ginger, cut into thin strips

2 teaspoons Asian fish sauce

1 teaspoon packed brown sugar

½ teaspoon five-spice powder

¼ cup thinly sliced fresh basil

▲ 2 Thai chile peppers, seeded and thinly sliced (optional)

1 Place noodles in large bowl. Add enough hot water to cover; let stand until noodles are soft, about 10 minutes. Drain in colander and rinse with cold water. Drain again.

2 Spray Dutch oven with nonstick spray and set over medium-high heat. Add steak and cook until instant-read thermometer inserted in side of steak registers 145°F for medium, 3–4 minutes per side. Transfer steak to cutting board and loosely cover with foil; let stand 5 minutes. Cut steak across grain into 16 slices.

3 Meanwhile, add broth and water to Dutch oven; bring to boil. Add radishes, scallions, ginger, fish sauce, brown sugar, and five-spice powder; bring to boil. Reduce heat and simmer, stirring occasionally, until vegetables are crisp-tender, about 5 minutes.

4 Evenly divide noodles among 4 bowls. Top each serving with 4 steak slices. Spoon broth and vegetables over noodles and beef; sprinkle with basil and chiles (if using).

PER SERVING (generous 1 cup broth, ½ cup noodles, and 4 slices steak): 313 Cal, 8 g Total Fat, 3 g Sat Fat, 0 g Trans Fat, 42 mg Chol, 351 mg Sod, 31 g Carb, 4 g Sugar, 1 g Fib, 29 g Prot, 64 mg Calc.

LEMONGRASS PORK SATAY WITH SPICY CUCUMBER SALAD

SERVES 4

▲ 3 Kirby cucumbers, thinly sliced

2 tablespoons chopped fresh mint

2 tablespoons seasoned rice vinegar

½ teaspoon Asian (dark) sesame oil

½ teaspoon toasted sesame seeds

¼ teaspoon red pepper flakes

▲ 1 (1-pound) pork tenderloin, trimmed and cut diagonally into ¼-inch-thick slices

1 shallot, minced

1 tablespoon minced lemongrass

2 tablespoons oyster sauce

1 teaspoon Thai red curry paste

① Combine cucumbers, mint, vinegar, oil, sesame seeds, and pepper flakes in medium bowl and toss to coat.

② Spray grill rack lightly with nonstick spray; preheat grill to medium-high or prepare medium-hot fire.

③ Combine pork, shallot, lemongrass, oyster sauce, and curry paste in large bowl and toss. Thread pork onto 4 (12-inch) metal skewers. Place skewers on grill rack and grill, turning frequently, until cooked through, about 4 minutes. Serve with cucumber salad.

PER SERVING (1 skewer and ½ cup cucumber salad): 169 Cal, 4 g Total Fat, 1 g Sat Fat, 0 g Trans Fat, 62 mg Chol, 344 mg Sod, 8 g Carb, 3 g Sugar, 3 g Fib, 25 g Prot, 62 mg Calc.

FYI

If you like, add a diced red or yellow bell pepper to the cucumber salad.

ROASTED BARBECUE PORK
WITH FRESH KIMCHI

ROASTED BARBECUE PORK WITH FRESH KIMCHI

SERVES 4

▲ ½ head Napa cabbage, shredded (about 4 cups)

▲ 1 cup shredded carrot

▲ 3 scallions, thinly sliced

2 tablespoons rice vinegar

1 tablespoon pickled ginger, finely chopped

1 tablespoon liquid from jar of pickled ginger

2 tablespoons Sriracha or other chili sauce

1 tablespoon reduced-sodium soy sauce

2 teaspoons hoisin sauce

▲ 1 (1-pound) pork tenderloin, trimmed

❶ To make kimchi, combine cabbage, carrot, scallions, vinegar, ginger, ginger juice, and 1 tablespoon Sriracha in large bowl and toss. Let stand at least 10 minutes for flavors to blend.

❷ Preheat oven to 425°F. Spray small shallow roasting pan with nonstick spray.

❸ Whisk together soy sauce, hoisin sauce, and remaining 1 tablespoon Sriracha in small bowl. Brush mixture over pork. Place pork in pan and roast until instant-read thermometer inserted into center of pork registers 145°F for medium, about 15 minutes. Transfer pork to cutting board and let stand 10 minutes. Cut pork into 12 slices and serve with kimchi.

PER SERVING (3 slices pork with ¾ cup kimchi):
168 Cal, 3 g Total Fat, 1 g Sat Fat, 0 g Trans Fat, 62 mg Chol, 359 mg Sod, 9 g Carb, 4 g Sugar, 2 g Fib, 24 g Prot, 67 mg Calc.

4 PointsPlus® value

FYI

Serve this spicy dish wrapped in lettuce leaves and sprinkled with thinly sliced scallion tops if you like. Try it with a side of nutty quinoa as well; a ⅔-cup portion of cooked quinoa per serving will increase the *PointsPlus* value by *3*.

CHICKEN BANH MI SANDWICHES

SERVES 4

▲ 1 cup shredded carrots

▲ 2 tablespoons pickled sliced jalapeño peppers (no added sugar), drained

¼ cup fresh cilantro leaves

2 teaspoons rice vinegar

½ teaspoon Asian (dark) sesame oil

▲ 1 pound ground skinless chicken breast

▲ 2 scallions, finely chopped

1 tablespoon reduced-sodium soy sauce

2 garlic cloves, minced

½ cup fat-free mayonnaise

1 tablespoon Sriracha or other chili sauce

1 (12-ounce) whole wheat baguette

① Combine carrots, jalapeño peppers, cilantro, vinegar, and sesame oil in small bowl.

② Stir together chicken, scallions, soy sauce, and garlic in medium bowl, mixing just until combined. With damp hands, shape mixture into 8 (½-inch-thick) patties.

③ Spray large nonstick skillet with nonstick spray and set over medium-high heat. Add patties and cook until browned and instant-read thermometer inserted in side of patties registers 165°F, 6–7 minutes per side.

④ Stir together mayonnaise and Sriracha in small bowl. Split baguette without cutting completely through. Remove small amount of soft center from baguette and discard, or save for bread crumbs. Cut into 4 equal pieces. Spread 2 tablespoons mayonnaise mixture on cut-sides of pieces. Stuff each with 2 patties and top with ¼ cup carrot mixture.

PER SERVING (1 sandwich): 399 Cal, 6 g Total Fat, 1 g Sat Fat, 0 g Trans Fat, 66 mg Chol, 974 mg Sod, 53 g Carb, 8 g Sugar, 6 g Fib, 33 g Prot, 31 mg Calc.

CHICKEN BANH MI
SANDWICHES

KOREAN-STYLE SWEET-AND-SPICY CHICKEN ROLLS

SERVES 4

▲ 2 **large egg whites**

2 **teaspoons Chinese-style hot mustard**

¾ **cup whole wheat panko (Japanese bread crumbs)**

2 **tablespoons sesame seeds**

▲ 1½ **pounds chicken tenders**

¼ **cup sake**

3 **tablespoons reduced-sodium soy sauce**

2 **teaspoons honey**

1 **garlic clove, minced**

½ **teaspoon hot chili oil**

▲ 8 **large green leaf lettuce leaves**

① Preheat oven to 425°F. Spray large rimmed baking sheet with nonstick spray.

② Whisk together egg whites and mustard in pie plate until frothy. Combine panko and sesame seeds on sheet of wax paper. Dip chicken tenders, one at a time, into egg white mixture; then into panko mixture, pressing to adhere. Place chicken in single layer on baking sheet; lightly spray with nonstick spray. Bake until golden and cooked through, 18–20 minutes.

③ Meanwhile, combine sake, soy sauce, honey, garlic, and chili oil in small bowl. Place lettuce leaves on work surface and top each with one eighth of chicken. Sprinkle each portion with about 1 tablespoon sauce and roll up lettuce to enclose chicken.

PER SERVING (2 rolls): 374 Cal, 8 g Total Fat, 1 g Sat Fat, 0 g Trans Fat, 94 mg Chol, 553 mg Sod, 30 g Carb, 14 g Sugar, 3 g Fib, 42 g Prot, 60 mg Calc.

FYI

For crunch and color, add 1 cup coleslaw mix and ¼ cup cilantro leaves to the rolls before enclosing the filling.

CRISPY TUNA WITH APRICOT-WASABI SAUCE

SERVES 4 • READY IN 20 MIN OR LESS

¼ cup apricot fruit spread

2 tablespoons orange juice

Juice of ½ lime

1 teaspoon wasabi paste

¼ teaspoon Asian (dark) sesame oil

25 plain rice crackers, broken into pieces

▲ 4 (5-ounce) tuna steaks

½ teaspoon salt

▲ 2 large egg whites

2 teaspoons cornstarch

1½ teaspoons canola oil

❶ Combine fruit spread, orange juice, lime juice, wasabi, and sesame oil in small bowl.

❷ Place crackers in food processor and pulse until finely crumbled (you should have about ¹/₂ cup crumbs); transfer to sheet of wax paper.

❸ Sprinkle tuna with salt. Whisk together egg whites and cornstarch in pie plate. Dip tuna, one piece at a time, into egg white mixture; then into cracker crumbs, pressing to adhere.

❹ Heat oil in large nonstick skillet over medium-high heat. Lightly spray tuna with nonstick spray. Place in skillet and cook until crust is golden and center is lightly pink, 2–3 minutes per side. Serve with apricot sauce.

PER SERVING (1 tuna steak and 2 tablespoons sauce):
398 Cal, 12 g Total Fat, 2 g Sat Fat, 0 g Trans Fat, 54 mg Chol, 472 mg Sod, 33 g Carb, 12 g Sugar, 3 g Fib, 38 g Prot, 35 mg Calc.

THAI SALMON IN CURRY BROTH

SERVES 4 • READY IN 20 MIN OR LESS

2   tablespoons unsweetened shredded coconut

1   (2-inch) piece fresh peeled ginger, coarsely chopped

2   garlic cloves, coarsely chopped

1   teaspoon canola oil

1   teaspoon mustard seeds

▲ 1   cup canned fire-roasted tomatoes

▲ 1   cup reduced-sodium chicken broth

½   cup light (reduced-fat) coconut milk

1   tablespoon packed brown sugar

▲ ¾   pound skinless wild salmon fillet, cut into 1-inch chunks

▲ 1   yellow bell pepper, diced

¼   cup chopped fresh cilantro

❶ Combine coconut, ginger, and garlic in mini-food processor or blender; pulse to make a paste.

❷ Heat oil in large nonstick skillet over medium heat. Add mustard seeds and cook, stirring frequently, until seeds just begin to pop, about 1 minute. Add coconut mixture and cook, stirring constantly, until fragrant, 1 minute. Add tomatoes, broth, coconut milk, and brown sugar; bring to boil. Reduce heat and simmer, uncovered, stirring occasionally, until flavors blend, about 10 minutes.

❸ Add salmon and bell pepper. Simmer until salmon is just opaque in center and bell pepper is crisp-tender, 2–3 minutes. Remove from heat and stir in cilantro.

PER SERVING (1 cup): 242 Cal, 12 g Total Fat, 3 g Sat Fat, 0 g Trans Fat, 54 mg Chol, 207 mg Sod, 13 g Carb, 6 g Sugar, 1 g Fib, 22 g Prot, 39 mg Calc.

THAI SALMON IN
CURRY BROTH

SHRIMP AND PINEAPPLE CURRY

SERVES 4 • READY IN 20 MIN OR LESS

- **2** teaspoons canola oil
- **1** tablespoon minced peeled fresh ginger
- **3** garlic cloves, minced
- **1** teaspoon Thai green curry paste
- **1** teaspoon ground cumin
- ▲ **1** pound large shrimp, peeled and deveined
- **½** cup light (reduced-fat) coconut milk
- **½** cup unsweetened pineapple juice
- **2** teaspoons Asian fish sauce
- ▲ **½** pound snow peas
- ▲ **2** cups fresh pineapple chunks
- **½** cup chopped fresh cilantro

1 Heat oil in large nonstick skillet over medium-high heat. Add ginger, garlic, curry paste, and cumin. Cook, stirring constantly, until fragrant, about 1 minute. Add shrimp and cook, stirring, until shrimp turn pink, 1–2 minutes.

2 Add coconut milk, pineapple juice, and fish sauce; bring to boil. Reduce heat. Add snow peas and pineapple chunks. Cook, stirring occasionally, until snow peas turn bright green and pineapple is heated through, about 1 minute. Remove from heat; stir in cilantro.

PER SERVING (1¼ cups): 216 Cal, 6 g Total Fat, 0 g Sat Fat, 0 g Trans Fat, 168 mg Chol, 472 mg Sod, 22 g Carb, 14 g Sugar, 3 g Fib, 21 g Prot, 83 mg Calc.

FYI

Serve this curry with a ⅔-cup portion of cooked brown rice per person and increase the *PointsPlus* value by *3.*

SAIGON SEAFOOD POT

SERVES 4 • READY IN 20 MIN OR LESS

4   ounces soba noodles

2   teaspoons canola oil

4   shallots, thinly sliced

4   garlic cloves, minced

½   teaspoon red pepper flakes

▲   1½ cups reduced-sodium chicken broth

▲   1   cup canned diced tomatoes

½   cup sake

2   teaspoons Asian fish sauce

▲   2   dozen littleneck clams, scrubbed

▲   2   pounds mussels, scrubbed and debearded

½   cup chopped fresh basil leaves

❶ Cook noodles according to package directions, omitting salt. Drain.

❷ Heat oil in large nonstick saucepan over medium heat. Add shallots, garlic, and pepper flakes; cook, stirring, until fragrant, 1–2 minutes. Add broth, tomatoes, sake, and fish sauce; bring to boil. Add clams. Cover and cook until clams open, about 5 minutes. Add mussels; cover and cook until mussels open, about 4 minutes. Discard any clams and mussels that do not open.

❸ Divide noodles among 4 bowls and top evenly with clams, mussels, and broth. Sprinkle with basil.

PER SERVING (½ cup noodles, about 12 mussels, 6 clams, and ¾ cup broth): 340 Cal, 5 g Total Fat, 1 g Sat Fat, 0 g Trans Fat, 52 mg Chol, 839 mg Sod, 38 g Carb, 3 g Sugar, 1 g Fib, 28 g Prot, 118 mg Calc.

OURS vs. THEIRS

Southeast Asia's vibrant flavors and diverse ingredients are captivating, and our satisfying recipes for many favorite dishes help you enjoy them at home quickly and easily. Here's how some of our elegant classics match up against dishes you might find at local restaurants.

YOUR CHOICE	OURS	THEIRS	WITH YOUR SAVINGS TRY
APPETIZER ROLLS	Two of our Summer Rolls with Crab and Mango, p. 181: **5 PointsPlus** value	Two (4-inch) restaurant-style Thai Spring Rolls: **10 PointsPlus** value	½ cup rice pudding: **5 PointsPlus** value
KOREAN BARBECUE	A serving of our Korean Steak Kebabs with Spicy Cilantro Sauce, p. 182: **5 PointsPlus** value	One (4-ounce) serving of restaurant-style Korean barbecue beef: **7 PointsPlus** value	2 tablespoons peanut satay sauce with cucumber sticks: **2 PointsPlus** value
SATAY	A serving of our Lemongrass Pork Satay with Spicy Cucumber Salad, p. 185: **4 PointsPlus** value	Two skewers of restaurant-style chicken satay with ¼ cup peanut sauce: **12 PointsPlus** value	1 cup Oriental (bean thread) noodles with soy sauce and 16 chopped peanuts: **8 PointsPlus** value total
THAI CURRY	A serving of our Thai Salmon in Curry Broth, p. 192: **6 PointsPlus** value	A 1-cup portion of restaurant-style chicken panang curry: **13 PointsPlus** value	A serving of our Green Papaya Salad, p. 180, and 2 of our Summer Rolls with Crab and Mango, p. 181: **7 PointsPlus** value total
PAD THAI	A 1-cup serving of our Vegetable Pad Thai, p. 197: **4 PointsPlus** value	A 1-cup serving of restaurant chicken and shrimp pad thai: **10 PointsPlus** value	2 (½-cup) scoops mango sorbet topped with 2 tablespoons sliced almonds: **6 PointsPlus** value total

VEGETABLE PAD THAI

SERVES 6

4   ounces flat rice stick noodles

2   teaspoons canola oil

▲ 1   red bell pepper, cut into thin strips

▲ 1   cup shredded carrots

▲ 6   scallions, thinly sliced

▲ 2   Thai chile peppers, thinly sliced

2   garlic cloves, minced

2   tablespoons Asian fish sauce

1   tablespoon packed brown sugar

1   tablespoon reduced-sodium soy sauce

▲ 1   cup bean sprouts

▲ ½   (14-ounce) container firm tofu, drained and cut into 1-inch chunks

½   cup chopped fresh cilantro

2   tablespoons dry-roasted peanuts, coarsely chopped

❶ Place noodles in large bowl. Add enough hot water to cover; let stand until noodles are soft, about 10 minutes. Drain in colander and rinse with cold water. Drain again.

❷ Heat oil in large nonstick skillet over medium-high heat. Add bell pepper, carrots, scallions, chile peppers, and garlic. Cook, stirring frequently, until vegetables are soft, about 5 minutes. Add fish sauce, brown sugar, and soy sauce; cook, stirring, until sugar dissolves, about 30 seconds. Add noodles, bean sprouts, and tofu. Cook, tossing gently to mix, until heated through, 2–3 minutes. Remove from heat; sprinkle with cilantro and peanuts.

PER SERVING (generous 1 cup noodles and 1 teaspoon peanuts): 160 Cal, 5 g Total Fat, 1 g Sat Fat, 0 g Trans Fat, 0 mg Chol, 571 mg Sod, 25 g Carb, 5 g Sugar, 2 g Fib, 5 g Prot, 94 mg Calc.

PointsPlus® value 4

CHAPTER 9

Flavors of India

Appetizers

LENTIL MULLIGATAWNY SOUP WITH PAPADAMS

BANANA-COCONUT RAITA

MANGO SALAD WITH LIME AND GINGER

Main Courses

GRILLED SPICED BEEF KEBABS IN NAAN

LAMB VINDALOO WITH POTATOES

CHICKEN TIKKA MASALA

CHICKEN KORMA WITH CAULIFLOWER

SPICY GRILLED CHICKEN LEGS WITH SAFFRON RICE

GOAN CHICKEN CURRY

TANDOORI-STYLE GRILLED SHRIMP WITH CARDAMOM BROWN RICE

SHRIMP AND TOMATO CURRY

BAKED FISH AND CLAMS WITH CILANTRO-MINT SAUCE

SPICY CHANA MASALA WITH SWEET POTATO

SAAG PANEER WITH PEAS

VEGETABLE BIRIYANI

Indian Pantry Partners

KEEP THESE STAPLES ON HAND TO QUICKLY GET HEALTHFUL MEALS ON THE TABLE.

Black Mustard Seeds Sometimes called brown mustard seeds, these pungent, crunchy seeds are popular in Indian curries and stews. You can substitute yellow mustard seeds, if you like, or simply omit them from the recipe.

Cardamom Both ground cardamom and whole cardamom pods are frequently used to bring warm flavor and tantalizing aroma to Indian curries and rice dishes. Whole pods are unpleasant to bite into, so be sure to remove and discard them before you serve your dishes.

Coconut Milk Rich, naturally sweet coconut milk is a staple ingredient in Indian cuisine, and it's particularly favored in South Indian recipes. Light (reduced-fat) coconut milk provides nutty flavor and creaminess with much less fat than regular coconut milk.

Cinnamon Sticks Cinnamon is a classic spice in many savory Indian dishes, and sticks (as opposed to the ground spice) deliver mild, fresh flavor and aroma without overwhelming the other seasonings in recipes. In a pinch, substitute ⅛ teaspoon ground cinnamon for each stick.

Garam Masala This ubiquitous blend of ground dry-roasted spices may include cloves, coriander, cumin, cardamom, fennel, black pepper, cinnamon, and more. It's available in the spice section of most supermarkets or at specialty stores.

Indian Chile Powder Made from ground dried red chiles, this fiery powder is the top choice for adding instant heat to Indian dishes. You can purchase it at Indian grocery stores or online from spice specialists. Cayenne is a good substitute and packs a similar punch of heat.

Lentils ▲ Lentils are popular in Indian vegetarian dishes for their meatlike flavor and high-protein content. Canned lentils are super convenient, although most varieties cook from dry in about 30 minutes. Red or yellow lentils are the classics for dishes like dahl and vegetarian mulligatawny soup, but you can use any color lentil without a major change in taste.

Paneer Cheese This fresh, mild, pleasantly spongy cheese is used as a delicious source of protein in many Indian vegetarian dishes. You'll find it in Indian groceries and some specialty stores.

Tandoori Spice A.k.a. tandoori masala, this mixture of dried spices and aromatics is blended specifically to be mixed with yogurt and used as a marinade. Blends vary from brand to brand but typically include chiles, garlic, cayenne, cumin, cloves, coriander, and more. Large supermarkets and Asian grocery stores usually carry at least one brand of tandoori spice.

LENTIL MULLIGATAWNY SOUP WITH PAPADAMS

SERVES 4 AS AN APPETIZER • READY IN 20 MIN OR LESS

¾ teaspoon canola oil

▲ 1 small onion, finely chopped

2 garlic cloves, finely chopped

1 teaspoon grated peeled fresh ginger

1 teaspoon ground coriander

½ teaspoon ground turmeric

⅛ teaspoon Indian chile powder
or cayenne

▲ 1½ cups low-sodium vegetable broth

▲ 1 (14-ounce) can lentils, rinsed and
drained

▲ 1½ cups canned, drained, no-salt-added
diced tomatoes

¼ teaspoon salt

½ cup water

4 store-bought papadams

½ lemon, cut into 4 wedges

1 Heat oil in large saucepan over high heat. Add onion, garlic, and ginger. Cook, stirring frequently, until onion softens, about 3 minutes. Add coriander, turmeric, and chile powder and cook 1 minute. Stir in broth, lentils, tomatoes, salt, and water; bring to boil. Reduce heat and simmer, uncovered, until flavors blend, about 10 minutes.

2 Meanwhile, preheat broiler. Lightly spray papadams with nonstick spray and place on baking sheet. Broil just until browned, about 30 seconds. Flip papadams with tongs and brown other side. (Watch very carefully so they don't burn.)

3 Divide soup among 4 bowls; squeeze lemon wedge over each. Serve with papadams.

PER SERVING (generous 1 cup soup and 1 papadam): 184 Cal, 2 g Total Fat, 0 g Sat Fat, 0 g Trans Fat, 0 mg Chol, 433 mg Sod, 31 g Carb, 8 g Sugar, 10 g Fib, 11 g Prot, 31 mg Calc.

BANANA-COCONUT RAITA

SERVES 6 AS AN APPETIZER • READY IN 20 MIN OR LESS

▲ **1 cup plain fat-free Greek yogurt**

▲ **1 banana, peeled and finely diced**

3 tablespoons unsweetened grated dried coconut

3 tablespoons chopped fresh mint or cilantro

Pinch Indian chile powder or cayenne

Stir together all ingredients in small bowl. Serve immediately, or cover and chill up to 1 day.

PER SERVING (¼ cup): 58 Cal, 2 g Total Fat, 2 g Sat Fat, 0 g Trans Fat, 0 mg Chol, 15 mg Sod, 7 g Carb, 4 g Sugar, 1 g Fib, 4 g Prot, 28 mg Calc.

2 PointsPlus® value ™

FYI

Try this naturally sweet, cooling raita as a dip for cucumbers sticks. It's also excellent served on the side with spicy dishes like our Lamb Vindaloo with Potatoes (page 207) or Spicy Grilled Chicken Legs with Saffron Rice (page 210).

Flavors of India

MANGO SALAD WITH LIME AND GINGER

SERVES 4 AS AN APPETIZER • READY IN 20 MIN OR LESS

Juice of 1 lime

1 teaspoon grated peeled fresh ginger

1 teaspoon honey

¼ teaspoon salt

▲ 2 large firm (not ripe) mangos, peeled, pit removed, and flesh very thinly sliced

▲ 2 Kirby cucumbers, halved and thinly sliced

▲ 1 large carrot, grated

1 cup lightly packed fresh cilantro leaves

½ teaspoon toasted cumin seeds (optional)

Whisk together lime juice, ginger, honey, and salt in large bowl. Add mango, cucumber, carrot, and cilantro and toss to coat with dressing. Sprinkle with cumin seeds (if using) and serve.

PER SERVING (1¼ cups): 99 Cal, 0 g Total Fat, 0 g Sat Fat, 0 g Trans Fat, 0 mg Chol, 161 mg Sod, 25 g Carb, 19 g Sugar, 4 g Fib, 2 g Prot, 51 mg Calc.

FYI

For a unique presentation, use a vegetable peeler or mandolin to slice the cucumbers, carrot, and peeled mangos lengthwise into long, thin, ribbonlike strips.

MANGO SALAD WITH
LIME AND GINGER

GRILLED SPICED BEEF KEBABS IN NAAN

SERVES 4 • READY IN 20 MIN OR LESS

▲ 1   pound lean ground beef (7% fat or less)

▲ 3   tablespoons grated onion

  2   tablespoons finely chopped fresh
       cilantro + more for garnish

  ¾   teaspoon garam masala

  ½   teaspoon salt

  ⅛   teaspoon Indian chile powder
       or cayenne

  1   (8.8-ounce) package whole-grain
       naan (2 pieces), warmed

❶ Combine beef, onion, cilantro, garam masala, salt, and chile powder in large bowl; fold ingredients together with hands or large rubber spatula. Evenly divide into 8 balls and roll each into thick sausage shape. Thread 2 pieces on each of 4 metal skewers; gently press meat so it adheres firmly to skewer.

❷ Heat ridged grill pan over high heat or preheat grill to medium high. Spray kebabs with nonstick spray. Grill, turning 3–4 times, until meat is browned on all sides and just cooked through, 8–10 minutes in grill pan or 6–8 minutes on grill.

❸ Meanwhile, warm naan according to package directions, omitting any fat. Cut each piece in half. Serve kebabs with naan.

PER SERVING (1 kebab and ½ naan): 329 Cal, 8 g Total Fat, 3 g Sat Fat, 0 g Trans Fat, 69 mg Chol, 584 mg Sod, 33 g Carb, 2 g Sugar, 6 g Fib, 30 g Prot, 24 mg Calc.

FYI

Naan is a delicious traditional Indian flatbread that's now readily available in supermarkets. If you can't find it, however, 1 pocketless pita per serving can be substituted with no change in *PointsPlus* value.

LAMB VINDALOO WITH POTATOES

SERVES 4

1   pound lean leg of lamb, trimmed, cut into ½-inch cubes

¼   teaspoon salt

1   teaspoon canola oil

▲ 1   small onion, diced

3   garlic cloves, finely chopped

½   teaspoon ground cumin

¼   teaspoon ground coriander

¼   teaspoon ground turmeric

¼   teaspoon Indian chile powder or cayenne

▲ ½   pound small red potatoes, quartered

¾   cup light (reduced-fat) coconut milk

1   teaspoon red wine vinegar

¼   cup water

Chopped fresh cilantro for garnish

❶ Sprinkle lamb with salt. Heat oil in large skillet over high heat. Add lamb and cook, stirring frequently, until lightly browned, about 4 minutes. Remove lamb from skillet and set aside. Add onion and garlic to skillet and cook, stirring, until softened, about 3 minutes.

❷ Stir in cumin, coriander, turmeric, and chile powder. Stir in potatoes, coconut milk, vinegar, and water; bring to boil. Reduce heat, cover, and simmer, stirring occasionally, until potatoes are tender, about 15 minutes.

❸ Stir in lamb and cook until heated through. Sprinkle with cilantro.

PER SERVING (1 cup): 335 Cal, 16 g Total Fat, 5 g Sat Fat, 0 g Trans Fat, 119 mg Chol, 245 mg Sod, 14 g Carb, 1 g Sugar, 1 g Fib, 33 g Prot, 31 mg Calc.

Flavors of India

CHICKEN TIKKA MASALA

SERVES 4

▲ 1 **pound skinless boneless chicken breasts, cut into ¾-inch cubes**

½ **teaspoon salt**

1 **teaspoon canola oil**

▲ 1 **small onion, chopped**

▲ ½ **serrano chile, stemmed and seeded**

3 **garlic cloves, finely chopped**

1 **teaspoon finely chopped peeled fresh ginger**

¾ **cup water**

▲ ½ **cup tomato puree**

¼ **teaspoon ground turmeric**

¼ **teaspoon garam masala**

¼ **teaspoon sugar**

▲ ⅔ **cup fat-free half-and-half**

Fresh cilantro for garnish

❶ Sprinkle chicken with ¼ teaspoon salt. Heat canola oil in large nonstick skillet over medium-high heat. Add chicken and cook, stirring frequently, until lightly browned, about 5 minutes.

❷ Meanwhile, combine onion, chile, garlic, and ginger, and water in blender and puree. Pour over chicken and bring to boil. Stir in tomato puree, turmeric, garam masala, sugar, and remaining ¼ teaspoon salt. Reduce heat and simmer, uncovered, until flavors are blended, 8–10 minutes. Stir in half-and-half; remove from heat and sprinkle with cilantro.

PER SERVING (¾ cup): 181 Cal, 4 g Total Fat, 1 g Sat Fat, 0 g Trans Fat, 63 mg Chol, 387 mg Sod, 9 g Carb, 4 g Sugar, 1 g Fib, 25 g Prot, 73 mg Calc.

FYI

Cook a large batch of brown rice on the weekend to make recipes like this one come together quickly during the week. Refrigerate cooked rice in an airtight container up to 4 days. A ⅔-cup portion of cooked brown rice has a *PointsPlus* value of *3*.

CHICKEN KORMA WITH CAULIFLOWER

SERVES 4

⅓ cup raw cashews

▲ 1 cup low-sodium chicken broth

▲ 1 pound skinless boneless chicken
      breasts, cut into ¾-inch cubes

  ¼ teaspoon salt

  1 teaspoon peanut oil

▲ 1 onion, diced

  3 garlic cloves, finely chopped

  ½ teaspoon ground cumin

  ½ teaspoon ground turmeric

  ½ teaspoon black mustard seeds

  1 cinnamon stick

▲ 3 cups small cauliflower florets

❶ Combine cashews and broth in blender. Puree until very smooth, about 1 minute.

❷ Sprinkle chicken with salt. Heat oil in large nonstick skillet over high heat. Add chicken and cook, stirring frequently, until browned, about 5 minutes. Add onion and garlic and cook 2 minutes. Stir in cumin, turmeric, mustard seeds, and cinnamon stick and cook 1 minute. Pour in cashew mixture and add cauliflower. Partially cover skillet and simmer until cauliflower is tender, 6–8 minutes. Remove and discard cinnamon stick.

PER SERVING (1⅓ cups): 242 Cal, 9 g Total Fat, 2 g Sat Fat, 0 g Trans Fat, 63 mg Chol, 244 mg Sod, 12 g Carb, 5 g Sugar, 3 g Fib, 28 g Prot, 53 mg Calc.

Flavors of India

SPICY GRILLED CHICKEN LEGS WITH SAFFRON RICE

SERVES 4

1½ cups water

¾ cup basmati rice

Pinch saffron threads

2 whole cloves

1 teaspoon salt

▲ 2 tablespoons finely chopped onion

3 garlic cloves, finely chopped

1 teaspoon grated peeled fresh ginger

1 teaspoon garam masala

¼ teaspoon Indian chile powder or cayenne

3 tablespoons lemon juice

1 teaspoon canola oil

8 (3-ounce) skinless chicken drumsticks

Lemon wedges for serving

❶ Bring water to boil in small saucepan. Stir in rice, saffron, cloves, and ½ teaspoon salt. Reduce heat, cover, and simmer until water is just absorbed, about 18 minutes. Remove from heat and let stand, covered, 5–10 minutes.

❷ Meanwhile, heat ridged grill pan over high heat. Combine onion, garlic, ginger, garam masala, chile powder, lemon juice, canola oil, and remaining ½ teaspoon salt in large bowl. Add chicken and stir to coat. Place chicken in grill pan and grill, turning frequently, until cooked through, about 15 minutes.

❸ Remove cloves from rice and discard; fluff rice with fork. Serve chicken with rice and lemon wedges on the side.

PER SERVING (2 chicken legs and ½ cup rice): 257 Cal, 4 g Total Fat, 1 g Sat Fat, 0 g Trans Fat, 73 mg Chol, 597 mg Sod, 32 g Carb, 0 g Sugar, 1 g Fib, 22 g Prot, 36 mg Calc.

FYI

When you grill the chicken, grill some fresh asparagus alongside to serve as an accompaniment.

BANANA-COCONUT RAITA, PAGE 203,
AND SPICY GRILLED CHICKEN LEGS
WITH SAFFRON RICE

GOAN CHICKEN CURRY

SERVES 4

3 garlic cloves

1½ teaspoons finely chopped peeled
   fresh ginger

▲ 1 serrano chile, stemmed and seeded

1 teaspoon tamarind paste (remove
   seeds or stems before measuring)
   or 2 teaspoons lemon juice

½ cup water

1 pound skinless boneless chicken thighs,
   cut into ¾-inch cubes

¼ teaspoon salt

1 teaspoon peanut oil

▲ 1 small onion, chopped

1½ teaspoons madras curry powder

▲ 1 cup canned, drained diced tomatoes

▲ 1 green bell pepper, diced

⅔ cup light (reduced-fat) coconut milk

❶ Combine garlic, ginger, chile, tamarind, and water in blender and puree. Set aside.

❷ Sprinkle chicken with salt. Heat oil in large nonstick skillet over medium-high heat. Add chicken and cook, stirring, until just browned, about 5 minutes. Stir in onion and cook 2 minutes. Stir in curry powder. Stir in garlic mixture and bring to boil.

❸ Stir in tomatoes, bell pepper, and coconut milk. Partially cover skillet, reduce heat and simmer, stirring frequently, until bell pepper is tender and chicken is cooked through, about 5 minutes.

PER SERVING (1 cup): 239 Cal, 13 g Total Fat, 3 g Sat Fat, 0 g Trans Fat, 74 mg Chol, 363 mg Sod, 10 g Carb, 4 g Sugar, 2 g Fib, 22 g Prot, 36 mg Calc.

FYI

Curries from the state of Goa along India's southwest coast often feature a delicious combination of coconut milk and tomatoes. Basmati rice is the classic accompaniment, but you could also try this dish with nutty, quick-cooking millet. A ⅔-cup portion of cooked millet has a *PointsPlus* value of *3*.

TANDOORI-STYLE GRILLED SHRIMP WITH CARDAMOM BROWN RICE

SERVES 4 • READY IN 20 MIN OR LESS

▲ ½ cup plain fat-free Greek yogurt

2 teaspoons finely chopped peeled fresh ginger

1 garlic clove, finely chopped

1 tablespoon tandoori spice

2 teaspoons lemon juice

¾ teaspoon salt

▲ 1¼ pounds extra-large shrimp, peeled and deveined

1½ cups water

5 cardamom pods

▲ 1½ cups quick-cooking brown rice

2 tablespoons chopped fresh cilantro

❶ Stir together yogurt, ginger, garlic, tandoori spice, lemon juice, and ¼ teaspoon salt in large bowl. Add shrimp and toss to coat.

❷ Preheat grill to medium-high or preheat broiler. Thread shrimp on 4 (12-inch) metal skewers and lightly spray with nonstick spray. Place shrimp on grill rack or broiler pan. Grill, turning once, until browned and just opaque in center, about 6 minutes.

❸ Meanwhile, bring water and cardamom pods to boil in small saucepan. Stir in rice and remaining ½ teaspoon salt. Reduce heat, cover, and simmer until rice is tender, about 10 minutes. Remove from heat and discard cardamom pods. Add cilantro and fluff rice with fork. Serve with shrimp.

PER SERVING (about 6 shrimp and ⅔ cup rice):
237 Cal, 2 g Total Fat, 0 g Sat Fat, 0 g Trans Fat, 210 mg Chol, 696 mg Sod, 27 g Carb, 1 g Sugar, 2 g Fib, 28 g Prot, 80 mg Calc.

OURS vs. THEIRS

Love Indian food? Then you'll definitely want to try cooking it at home. Not only will our selection of favorite regional dishes fill your kitchen with the wonderful aromas of the cuisine's classic spices, but you'll enjoy them while sticking to your daily *PointsPlus* Target. Here's how a few popular dishes compare.

YOUR CHOICE	OURS	THEIRS	WITH YOUR SAVINGS TRY
LAMB VINDALOO	A serving of our Lamb Vindaloo with Potatoes, p. 207: *9 PointsPlus* value	A 1-cup serving of restaurant-style lamb vindaloo: *16 PointsPlus* value	A serving of our Lentil Mulligatawny Soup with Papadams, p. 202, and a serving of our Mango Salad with Lime and Ginger, p. 204: *7 PointsPlus* value total
CHICKEN KORMA	A serving of our Chicken Korma with Cauliflower, p. 209: *6 PointsPlus* value	A 1-cup serving of restaurant-style chicken korma: *15 PointsPlus* value	½ cup of our Banana-Coconut Raita, p. 203, and a 7 x 8-inch piece of naan bread: *9 PointsPlus* value total
CHICKEN CURRY	A serving of our Goan Chicken Curry, p. 212: *6 PointsPlus* value	1 cup of restaurant-style chicken curry: *10 PointsPlus* value	1¼-cup serving of mango lassi: *4 PointsPlus* value
CHANA MASALA	A serving of our Spicy Chana Masala with Sweet Potato, p. 218: *5 PointsPlus* value	1-cup serving of restaurant-style chana masala: *9 PointsPlus* value	1 scoop (½ cup) fat-free frozen yogurt sprinkled with 1 tablespoon sliced almonds *4 PointsPlus* value total
SAAG PANEER	A serving of our Saag Paneer with Peas, p. 219: *5 PointsPlus* value	A 1-cup serving of restaurant-style saag paneer: *8 PointsPlus* value	½ cup tapioca pudding topped with a sliced banana: *3 PointsPlus* value total

SHRIMP AND TOMATO CURRY

SERVES 4 • READY IN 20 MIN OR LESS

2   teaspoons olive oil

▲ 1   Vidalia or other sweet onion,
      thinly sliced

▲ 1   serrano pepper, seeded and diced

1   bay leaf

1½ teaspoons curry powder

4   garlic cloves, minced

▲ 1¼ pounds large shrimp, peeled and
      deveined

▲ 4   medium tomatoes (about 1⅓ pounds),
      seeded and chopped

1   tablespoon lime juice

2   tablespoons fresh cilantro leaves

❶ Heat oil in large nonstick skillet over medium-high heat. Add onion and cook, stirring, until softened, about 3 minutes. Stir in serrano pepper, bay leaf, and curry powder. Reduce heat to medium and stir in garlic and shrimp. Cover and cook until shrimp is just opaque, 3–4 minutes.

❷ Stir in tomatoes. Cover and cook just until tomatoes soften, about 5 minutes. Remove and discard bay leaf. Stir in lime juice and cilantro leaves.

PER SERVING (about 1¼ cups): 181 Cal, 4 g Total Fat, 1 g Sat Fat, 0 g Trans Fat, 210 mg Chol, 255 mg Sod, 12 g Carb, 8 g Sugar, 2 g Fib, 25 g Prot, 77 mg Calc.

FYI

Rice is the classic partner for spicy curries, but you might want to try couscous for a change. Whole wheat couscous is ready in less than 10 minutes; a ⅔-cup serving has a *PointsPlus* value of **3.**

Flavors of India

BAKED FISH AND CLAMS
WITH CILANTRO-MINT SAUCE

BAKED FISH AND CLAMS WITH CILANTRO-MINT SAUCE

SERVES 4

▲ 4 (¼-pound) pieces skinless cod fillet

¼ teaspoon salt

▲ 12 cockles or other small clams, scrubbed

½ cup light (reduced-fat) coconut milk

3 garlic cloves

▲ ½ jalapeño pepper, seeded, or to taste

½ teaspoon garam masala

¼ teaspoon black mustard seeds

▲ ½ cup plain fat-free Greek yogurt

¼ cup chopped fresh cilantro

¼ cup chopped fresh mint

½ teaspoon sugar

Pinch Indian chile powder or cayenne

❶ Preheat oven to 425°F. Spray 8 x 12-inch baking pan with nonstick spray. Sprinkle fish with salt and place in pan. Arrange cockles around fish.

❷ Combine coconut milk, garlic, jalapeño, garam masala, and mustard seeds in blender and pulse until fairly smooth. Pour mixture over fish and clams. Bake until fish is just opaque in center and clams open, 12–15 minutes.

❸ Meanwhile, combine yogurt, cilantro, mint, sugar, and chile powder in small bowl. Divide fish and clams among 4 plates or bowls (discard any clams that did not open) and spoon pan juices over each serving. Top with 2 tablespoons yogurt sauce.

PER SERVING (1 piece fish, 3 clams, 2 tablespoons pan juices, and 2 tablespoons yogurt sauce): 200 Cal, 5 g Total Fat, 1 g Sat Fat, 0 g Trans Fat, 68 mg Chol, 270 mg Sod, 6 g Carb, 2 g Sugar, 0 g Fib, 32 g Prot, 66 mg Calc.

FYI

For color and flavor, garnish this dish with thinly sliced red and yellow bell peppers.

SPICY CHANA MASALA WITH SWEET POTATO

SERVES 4

1 teaspoon canola oil

▲ 1 small red onion, chopped

4 garlic cloves, chopped

1 teaspoon ground cumin

½ teaspoon paprika

½ teaspoon ground turmeric

½ teaspoon garam masala

¼ teaspoon ground Indian chile powder
or cayenne

2 tablespoons tomato paste

1 tablespoon lemon juice

¾ cup water

▲ 1 large (12-ounce) sweet potato, peeled
and cut into ½-inch cubes

¼ teaspoon salt

▲ 1 (15-ounce) can no-salt-added
chickpeas, rinsed and drained

Chopped fresh cilantro for garnish

❶ Heat oil in large skillet over medium-high heat. Add onion and garlic and cook, stirring frequently, until onion is soft, about 3 minutes. Stir in cumin, paprika, turmeric, garam masala, and chile powder. Stir in tomato paste, lemon juice, and water. Add sweet potato and salt; bring to boil. Reduce heat, cover, and simmer until sweet potato is tender, about 12 minutes.

❷ Stir in chickpeas and heat through. Serve garnished with cilantro.

PER SERVING (1⅓ cups): 213 Cal, 2 g Total Fat, 0 g Sat Fat, 0 g Trans Fat, 0 mg Chol, 286 mg Sod, 41 g Carb, 6 g Sugar, 8 g Fib, 8 g Prot, 86 mg Calc.

5 PointsPlus® value

SAAG PANEER WITH PEAS

SERVES 4 • READY IN 20 MIN OR LESS

1½ teaspoons canola oil

½ pound paneer cheese cubes

▲ 1 onion, diced

2 teaspoons chopped peeled fresh ginger

1 teaspoon black mustard seeds

½ teaspoon garam masala

⅛ teaspoon Indian chile powder or cayenne

½ cup water

½ teaspoon salt

▲ ¾ pound baby spinach leaves

▲ 1½ cups frozen peas

▲ ⅓ cup plain fat-free Greek yogurt

1 Heat oil in large nonstick skillet over high heat until very hot. Add paneer and cook, shaking skillet or stirring gently, just until cheese is browned, about 2 minutes. Carefully remove cheese from skillet and set aside.

2 Reduce heat to medium-high. Add onion and ginger to skillet. Cook, stirring, until onion is soft, about 3 minutes. Stir in mustard seeds, garam masala, and chile powder; cook, stirring, 1 minute. Stir in water and salt; bring to boil.

3 Stir in spinach leaves, a few handfuls at a time, stirring well after each addition. Stir in peas. Reduce heat to medium, cover, and cook until peas are heated through, about 4 minutes. Remove from heat and stir in yogurt.

PER SERVING (1¼ cups): 211 Cal, 10 g Total Fat, 5 g Sat Fat, 0 g Trans Fat, 0 mg Chol, 546 mg Sod, 20 g Carb, 6 g Sugar, 7 g Fib, 13 g Prot, 99 mg Calc.

5 PointsPlus value

FYI

Saag (braised greens) and lightly chewy paneer cheese are classics of Indian vegetarian cooking. For an extra *4 PointsPlus* value per serving, spoon each portion of this spinach dish over a large (5-inch-long) split baked russet potato or sweet potato.

VEGETABLE BIRIYANI

VEGETABLE BIRIYANI

SERVES 4

	1	teaspoon unsalted butter
▲	1	small red onion, sliced
	2	garlic cloves, sliced
	¾	cup basmati rice, rinsed
	1	cinnamon stick
	¼	teaspoon ground cardamom
▲	1½	cups low-sodium vegetable broth
	¼	teaspoon salt
	⅛	teaspoon Indian chile powder or cayenne
▲	1½	cups small cauliflower florets
▲	1	cup frozen peas
▲	1	cup sliced green beans
▲	1	tomato, diced
	⅓	cup golden raisins
	¼	cup sliced almonds

❶ Melt butter in large saucepan over medium-high heat. Add onion and garlic and cook, stirring occasionally, 2 minutes. Add rice, cinnamon stick, and cardamom; cook, stirring, 2 minutes. Add broth, salt, and chile powder. Bring to boil, stir once, reduce heat, cover, and simmer 5 minutes.

❷ Stir in cauliflower, peas, green beans, tomato, and raisins. Cover and cook, stirring once or twice, until vegetables are cooked through and rice is tender, about 15 minutes. Remove pan from heat and let stand, covered, 5 minutes. Serve garnished with almonds.

PER SERVING (1½ cups rice and vegetables and 1 tablespoon almonds): 282 Cal, 4 g Total Fat, 1 g Sat Fat, 0 g Trans Fat, 3 mg Chol, 246 mg Sod, 55 g Carb, 15 g Sugar, 7 g Fib, 8 g Prot, 83 mg Calc.

7 PointsPlus® value

FYI

Rice-based biriyani dishes are very popular in Northern India. Fluffy, aromatic basmati is key to the dish's flavor and texture. Basmati is sometimes coated with talc or other polishing agents so it's best to give it a quick rinse under cold water before cooking it.

CHAPTER 10

Bonus!
Weekend Treats

CUPCAKES, COOKIES,
AND COFFEEHOUSE FAVORITES

BLACK-AND-WHITE CUPCAKES

PUMPKIN CUPCAKES WITH CARAMEL FROSTING

ANGEL FOOD CUPCAKES WITH MARSHMALLOW FROSTING

PEACH COFFEE CAKE WITH CRUMB TOPPING

STREUSEL-TOPPED APPLE-BUTTERMILK MUFFINS

MORNING CARROT-ZUCCHINI MUFFINS

CHERRY-ORANGE BREAKFAST SCONES

CINNAMON ROLLS WITH CREAM CHEESE FROSTING

RASPBERRY-CHOCOLATE SHORTBREAD BARS

TRIPLE CHOCOLATE BROWNIES

CHOCOLATE-WALNUT BISCOTTI

MOLASSES SPICE AND RAISIN COOKIES

Weekend Treat Pantry Partners

KEEPING THESE STAPLES ON HAND WILL HELP YOU WHIP UP DELICIOUS GOODIES WHEN YOU HAVE A LITTLE EXTRA TIME.

Canned Pumpkin Puree ▲ It's not just for pie! Use pure canned pumpkin to bring deep flavor and a dose of veggie nutrition to a variety of baked goods.

Confectioners' Sugar A.k.a. powdered sugar, this finely ground sweetner is the standard for frostings and glazes. It's also terrific for sprinkling over baked goods like muffins or cakes to dress them up without additional frostings.

Fat-Free Buttermilk ▲ Cultured buttermilk is tangier, thicker, and richer in taste than regular fat-free milk. To make a substitute, combine 1 tablespoon lemon juice and 1 cup minus 1 tablespoon fat-free milk and let the mixture stand for 5 minutes.

Light Stick Butter This reduced-fat butter product comes in stick form for easy measuring.

Rolled Oats Oats are great for bringing flavor, texture, and whole-grain nutrition to everything from muffins to crumbles to cookies. We find quick-cooking oats to be the most versatile, although old-fashioned oats have a heartier texture that's sometimes better for toppings.

Semisweet Chocolate Chips Chocolate lovers are hard-pressed to find a better addition to cookies, brownies, and other sweet treats than chocolate chips. They're also convenient for melting. For variety, look for mini chocolate chips and white chocolate chips.

Unsweetened Cocoa Powder Cocoa powder packs intense chocolate flavor without adding additional fat or sugar to recipes. If possible, choose the darker Dutch process cocoa, a powder which has been treated with alkali to reduce cocoa's natural acidity.

Unsweetened Applesauce ▲ Applesauce contributes moisture, texture, and sweetness to many baked goods. Adding it to recipes can reduce the amount of fat required while still yielding tender results.

Whole Wheat Pastry Flour This finely milled flour is tops for adding whole wheat nutrition to baked goods. Its lighter texture makes everything from muffins to cookies more tender than if they were made with regular whole wheat flour.

Weekend Treats

BLACK-AND-WHITE CUPCAKES

SERVES 12

CUPCAKES

1 **cup cake flour**

½ **teaspoon baking powder**

¼ **teaspoon baking soda**

¼ **teaspoon salt**

10 **tablespoons granulated sugar**

3 **tablespoons unsweetened Dutch process cocoa**

2 **tablespoons water**

4 **tablespoons light stick butter, at room temperature**

1 **large egg, at room temperature**

1 **teaspoon vanilla extract**

½ **cup plain fat-free yogurt**

GLAZE

1 **ounce bittersweet chocolate, chopped**

1 **tablespoon low-fat (1%) milk**

¼ **cup confectioners' sugar**

1 To make cupcakes, preheat oven to 350°F. Line 12-cup muffin pan with paper liners. Whisk together flour, baking powder, baking soda, and salt in medium bowl. Whisk together 2 tablespoons granulated sugar, cocoa, and water in small bowl until smooth.

2 With electric mixer, beat butter in large bowl until creamy. Gradually beat in remaining 8 tablespoons sugar. Beat 2 minutes. Beat in egg and vanilla. With mixer on low speed, alternately add flour mixture and yogurt, beginning and ending with flour mixture. Beat just until blended. Stir ¾ cup of batter into cocoa mixture. Spoon half of vanilla batter into prepared muffin cups. Spoon cocoa batter over vanilla batter. Top with remaining vanilla batter. With table knife, cut and twist through batter to marble. Bake until toothpick inserted into centers of cupcakes comes out clean, 18–20 minutes. Cool in pan 5 minutes. Remove cupcakes from pan and cool completely on rack.

3 To make glaze, put chocolate and milk in small microwavable bowl. Microwave on High 30 seconds. Whisk gently until chocolate is melted. Whisk in confectioners' sugar. Spread glaze on cupcakes, using about 1 teaspoon per cupcake.

PER SERVING (1 iced cupcake): 111 Cal, 5 g Total Fat, 2 g Sat Fat, 0 g Trans Fat, 23 mg Chol, 133 mg Sod, 17 g Carb, 7 g Sugar, 0 g Fib, 3 g Prot, 32 mg Calc.

PUMPKIN CUPCAKES WITH CARAMEL FROSTING

SERVES 12

CUPCAKES

1	cup whole wheat pastry flour
1	teaspoon baking powder
1	teaspoon cinnamon
½	teaspoon ground ginger
½	teaspoon baking soda
½	teaspoon salt
1	cup canned pumpkin puree
⅔	cup granulated sugar
⅓	cup canola oil
2	large eggs
2	tablespoons light molasses

FROSTING

½	cup packed dark brown sugar
2	tablespoons light stick butter
2	tablespoons low-fat (1%) milk
½	cup confectioners' sugar
¼	teaspoon vanilla extract

❶ Preheat oven to 350°F. Line 12-cup muffin pan with paper liners.

❷ To make cupcakes, whisk together flour, baking powder, cinnamon, ginger, baking soda, and salt in small bowl. Whisk together pumpkin, sugar, oil, eggs, and molasses in large bowl. Add flour mixture to pumpkin mixture and whisk until smooth. Spoon batter into prepared muffin cups. Bake until toothpick inserted in centers comes out clean, about 20 minutes. Cool in pan 10 minutes. Remove cupcakes from pan and cool completely on rack.

❸ To make frosting, combine brown sugar, butter, and milk in small saucepan over medium heat. Cook, stirring occasionally, until mixture comes to boil. Boil 3 minutes. Remove from heat and let cool 30 minutes.

❹ Add confectioners' sugar and vanilla to brown sugar mixture. With an electric mixer on medium speed, beat until smooth. Spread thin layer of frosting on cooled cupcakes.

PER SERVING (1 frosted cupcake): 207 Cal, 8 g Total Fat, 2 g Sat Fat, 0 g Trans Fat, 38 mg Chol, 223 mg Sod, 33 g Carb, 25 g Sugar, 1 g Fib, 2 g Prot, 46 mg Calc.

6 PointsPlus value

Weekend Treats

ANGEL FOOD CUPCAKES WITH MARSHMALLOW FROSTING

SERVES 18

CUPCAKES

¾ cup cake flour

⅔ cup confectioners' sugar

▲ 8 large egg whites

¾ teaspoon cream of tartar

½ teaspoon salt

½ cup granulated sugar

1½ teaspoons vanilla extract

FROSTING

½ cup light corn syrup

2 teaspoons powdered egg whites

2 tablespoons water

½ teaspoon vanilla extract

Pinch salt

1 To make cupcakes, preheat oven to 350°F. Line 18 muffin cups with paper liners. Sift together flour and confectioners' sugar onto piece of wax paper. With electric mixer on high speed, beat egg whites, cream of tartar, and salt in large bowl until mixture forms soft peaks. Gradually beat in granulated sugar. Beat in vanilla. Sift half of flour mixture over beaten egg whites and fold in with rubber spatula. Repeat with remaining flour mixture.

2 Spoon batter into muffin cups, almost filling each; smooth tops with back of spoon. Bake until tops are golden and spring back when lightly pressed, 14–15 minutes. Cool in pan 5 minutes. Remove from pan and cool completely on rack.

3 To make frosting, with electric mixer on high speed, beat corn syrup, powdered egg whites, water, vanilla, and salt until mixture is very thick and fluffy, about 5 minutes. Frost cupcakes with small spatula.

PER SERVING (1 frosted cupcake): 75 Cal, 0 g Total Fat, 0 g Sat Fat, 0 g Trans Fat, 0 mg Chol, 106 mg Sod, 17 g Carb, 7 g Sugar, 0 g Fib, 2 g Prot, 3 mg Calc.

ANGEL FOOD CUPCAKES WITH MARSHMALLOW
FROSTING; BLACK-AND-WHITE CUPCAKES,
PAGE 226; PUMPKIN CUPCAKES WITH CARAMEL
FROSTING, PAGE 227.

PEACH COFFEE CAKE WITH CRUMB TOPPING

SERVES 16

CAKE

- 1¾ cups whole wheat pastry flour
- ½ cup packed brown sugar
- ½ teaspoon baking powder
- ¼ teaspoon baking soda
- ½ teaspoon salt
- 3 tablespoons unsalted butter, softened
- ⅓ cup granulated sugar
- ▲ ½ cup fat-free egg substitute
- ¾ cup vanilla low-fat yogurt
- ▲ 1 peach, pitted and diced

TOPPING

- ⅓ cup packed brown sugar
- ¼ cup whole wheat pastry flour
- 1 teaspoon cinnamon
- 2 tablespoons melted unsalted butter

1 Preheat oven to 350°F. Line 9-inch square baking pan with foil, extending foil over rim of pan by 2 inches. Spray foil with nonstick spray.

2 To make cake, whisk together flour and brown sugar in medium bowl. Whisk in baking powder, baking soda, and salt. With electric mixer beat butter and granulated sugar in large bowl until fluffy, about 4 minutes. Beat in egg substitute. With mixer on low speed, alternately add flour mixture and yogurt, beginning and ending with flour mixture, beating just until blended. Scrape half of batter (about 1½ cups) into prepared pan and spread evenly. Sprinkle with peach. Spoon on remaining batter and spread evenly.

3 To make topping, combine brown sugar, flour, and cinnamon in small bowl. Drizzle butter over top and stir with fork until blended. Sprinkle mixture over batter.

4 Bake until toothpick inserted in center of cake comes out clean, 30–35 minutes. Cool completely in pan on rack. Lift cake from pan using foil. Cut into 16 squares.

PER SERVING (1 square): 143 Cal, 4 g Total Fat, 2 g Sat Fat, 0 g Trans Fat, 10 mg Chol, 132 mg Sod, 25 g Carb, 16 g Sugar, 1 g Fib, 3 g Prot, 45 mg Calc.

STREUSEL-TOPPED APPLE-BUTTERMILK MUFFINS

SERVES 12

2 cups whole wheat pastry flour

1½ teaspoons baking powder

½ teaspoon baking soda

½ teaspoon salt

2 teaspoons cinnamon

▲ ¾ cup fat-free buttermilk

▲ ⅓ cup unsweetened applesauce

3 tablespoons pure maple syrup

▲ 2 large egg whites

½ cup + 2 tablespoons packed brown sugar

3 tablespoons canola oil

▲ 1 Granny Smith apple, peeled, cored, and chopped

3 tablespoons old-fashioned oats

2 tablespoons chopped walnuts

❶ Preheat oven to 400°F. Line 12-cup muffin pan with paper liners.

❷ Whisk together flour, baking powder, baking soda, salt, and 1½ teaspoons cinnamon in large bowl. Whisk together buttermilk, applesauce, maple syrup, egg whites, ½ cup brown sugar, and 2 tablespoons oil in medium bowl. Add to flour mixture and stir just until flour mixture is moistened. Fold in apple. Spoon batter into prepared muffin cups.

❸ Combine remaining ½ teaspoon cinnamon, 2 tablespoons brown sugar, and remaining 1 tablespoon oil in small bowl. Add oats and walnuts; mix with fingers until evenly moistened. Sprinkle oat mixture over batter, pressing lightly to adhere. Bake until toothpick inserted in centers comes out clean, about 20 minutes. Cool in pan on rack 10 minutes. Remove muffins from pan and cool completely on rack.

PER SERVING (1 muffin): 178 Cal, 5 g Total Fat, 0 g Sat Fat, 0 g Trans Fat, 0 mg Chol, 244 mg Sod, 32 g Carb, 17 g Sugar, 2 g Fib, 4 g Prot, 25 mg Calc.

Weekend Treats

MORNING CARROT-ZUCCHINI MUFFINS

SERVES 12

1   cup whole wheat pastry flour

¼   cup quick-cooking oats

1   teaspoon cinnamon

1   teaspoon baking soda

½   teaspoon baking powder

¼   teaspoon salt

⅓   cup packed brown sugar

3½ tablespoons canola oil

▲ 2   large eggs

1   teaspoon vanilla extract

▲ 1   small Granny Smith apple, peeled, cored, and shredded

▲ 1   medium carrot, shredded

▲ ½   cup shredded zucchini

½   cup raisins

❶ Preheat oven to 375°F. Line 12-cup muffin pan with paper liners.

❷ Whisk together flour, oats, cinnamon, baking soda, baking powder, and salt in medium bowl. Whisk together brown sugar, oil, eggs, and vanilla in large bowl. Stir in apple, carrot, zucchini, and raisins. Add flour mixture and stir just until combined.

❸ Spoon batter into prepared muffin cups. Bake until toothpick inserted in centers comes out clean, about 20 minutes. Cool in pan on rack 10 minutes. Remove muffins from pan and cool completely on rack.

PER SERVING (1 muffin): 139 Cal, 5 g Total Fat, 1 g Sat Fat, 0 g Trans Fat, 36 mg Chol, 183 mg Sod, 21 g Carb, 13 g Sugar, 2 g Fib, 3 g Prot, 25 mg Calc.

4 PointsPlus® value

CHERRY-ORANGE BREAKFAST SCONES

SERVES 8

¾ cup whole wheat pastry flour

¼ cup quick-cooking oats

2 tablespoons packed brown sugar

¾ teaspoon baking powder

¼ teaspoon baking soda

¼ teaspoon salt

2 tablespoons cold unsalted butter, cut into pieces

½ cup dried cherries

▲ ⅓ cup fat-free buttermilk

▲ 1 large egg white

1 teaspoon grated orange zest

6 tablespoons confectioners' sugar

2 teaspoons orange juice

❶ Preheat oven to 375°F. Spray baking sheet with nonstick spray.

❷ Whisk together flour, oats, brown sugar, baking powder, baking soda, and salt in large bowl. With pastry blender or 2 knives used scissor-fashion, cut in butter until mixture resembles fine crumbs. Stir in cherries. Whisk together buttermilk, egg white, and orange zest in small bowl. Add to flour mixture and stir just until soft dough forms.

❸ Gather dough into ball and place on lightly floured surface. Lightly knead two or three times. Press dough into 8-inch circle and cut into 8 wedges. Place wedges on prepared baking sheet, about 2 inches apart. Bake until toothpick inserted in centers comes out clean, about 15 minutes. Transfer scones to rack; cool 10 minutes.

❹ Stir together confectioners' sugar and orange juice in small bowl until smooth. Place sheet of wax paper under rack to catch drips. Drizzle glaze over scones and let stand until glaze sets, about 30 minutes.

PER SERVING (1 glazed scone): 140 Cal, 3 g Total Fat, 2 g Sat Fat, 0 g Trans Fat, 8 mg Chol, 182 mg Sod, 25 g Carb, 14 g Sugar, 2 g Fib, 3 g Prot, 38 mg Calc.

4 PointsPlus® value ™

Weekend Treats

CINNAMON ROLLS WITH
CREAM CHEESE FROSTING

CINNAMON ROLLS WITH CREAM CHEESE FROSTING

SERVES 12

FILLING

¼ **cup packed brown sugar**

¼ **cup granulated sugar**

2 **teaspoons cinnamon**

DOUGH

2½ **cups all-purpose flour**

3 **tablespoons granulated sugar**

1 **teaspoon baking powder**

½ **teaspoon baking soda**

½ **teaspoon salt**

▲ 1 **cup fat-free buttermilk**

▲ 1 **large egg**

3 **tablespoons unsalted butter, melted**

FROSTING

¾ **cup confectioners' sugar**

3 **tablespoons light cream cheese (Neufchâtel)**

▲ 1 **teaspoon fat-free buttermilk**

⅛ **teaspoon vanilla extract**

1 To make filling, combine all ingredients in small bowl.

2 To make dough, preheat oven to 425°F. Spray 9 x 13-inch baking dish with nonstick spray. Whisk together flour, granulated sugar, baking powder, baking soda, and salt in large bowl. Whisk together buttermilk, egg, and 2 tablespoons butter in small bowl. Add to flour mixture and stir until dough forms. Turn dough out onto floured surface and knead until smooth, about 30 seconds.

3 With floured rolling pin, roll out dough on floured surface to 12 x 9-inch rectangle. Brush dough with remaining 1 tablespoon butter and sprinkle with filling mixture. Tightly roll up dough from long side. Pinch seams to seal. Turn roll seam side down, and with serrated knife, cut into 12 slices. Arrange cut-side down in pan. Cover pan with foil. Bake 15 minutes. Remove foil and bake until rolls are golden, 12–14 minutes. Cool in pan 10 minutes.

4 To make frosting, with electric mixer, beat all ingredients in small bowl until smooth. Spread frosting on rolls. Let stand 15 minutes. Serve warm or at room temperature.

PER SERVING (1 roll): 208 Cal, 4 g Total Fat, 2 g Sat Fat, 0 g Trans Fat, 28 mg Chol, 238 mg Sod, 39 g Carb, 18 g Sugar, 1 g Fib, 4 g Prot, 53 mg Calc.

6 PointsPlus® value

Weekend Treats

RASPBERRY-CHOCOLATE SHORTBREAD BARS

SERVES 30

2   cups reduced-fat buttermilk baking mix

⅓   cup packed brown sugar

2   tablespoons unsalted butter, melted and cooled

▲ 2   tablespoons fat-free milk

1   (14-ounce) can fat-free sweetened condensed milk

1¼   cups semisweet chocolate chips

3   tablespoons chopped pecans

⅓   cup seedless raspberry preserves

❶ Preheat oven to 350°F. Line 9 x 13-inch baking pan with foil, extending foil over rim of pan by 2 inches. Spray foil with nonstick spray.

❷ Whisk together baking mix, brown sugar, and butter in large bowl. Transfer ¼ cup mixture to small bowl; set aside. Drizzle milk over mixture in large bowl and stir until evenly moistened. Turn into prepared pan and press to evenly cover bottom. Bake until edges brown, about 15 minutes.

❸ Put condensed milk and 1 cup chocolate chips in large microwavable bowl. Microwave on High 1 minute. Stir until chips are melted; microwave 10–15 seconds longer if necessary. Spread filling evenly over hot crust. Mix pecans into reserved crumb mixture. Sprinkle over filling. Spoon jam by ½ teaspoonfuls over filling, spacing about 2 inches apart. Sprinkle with remaining ¼ cup chocolate chips.

❹ Bake until filling is set and jam is bubbly, about 25 minutes. Cool completely in pan on rack. Lift from pan using foil. Cut into 30 bars.

PER SERVING (1 bar): 171 Cal, 5 g Total Fat, 2 g Sat Fat, 0 g Trans Fat, 4 mg Chol, 204 mg Sod, 29 g Carb, 19 g Sugar, 1 g Fib, 3 g Prot, 61 mg Calc.

TRIPLE CHOCOLATE BROWNIES

SERVES 16

⅔   cup all-purpose flour

¼   cup unsweetened cocoa powder

½   teaspoon baking powder

¼   teaspoon salt

⅓   cup light stick butter

2   ounces unsweetened chocolate, chopped

1   teaspoon instant espresso powder

¾   cup granulated sugar

¼   cup packed brown sugar

▲ 2   large eggs

1   teaspoon vanilla extract

⅓   cup semisweet chocolate chips

1 Preheat oven to 350°F. Line 9-inch square baking pan with foil, extending foil over rim of pan by 2 inches. Spray foil with nonstick spray.

2 Whisk together flour, cocoa, baking powder, and salt in small bowl; set aside. Melt butter, chocolate, and espresso powder in medium saucepan over low heat. Remove saucepan from heat. Whisk in granulated sugar and brown sugar. Whisk in eggs and vanilla. Stir in flour mixture and chocolate chips until combined. Scrape batter into prepared pan and spread evenly.

3 Bake until a toothpick inserted in center comes out with moist crumbs, 20–25 minutes. Cool completely in pan on rack. Lift from pan using foil. Cut into 16 squares.

PER SERVING (1 square): 133 Cal, 7 g Total Fat, 4 g Sat Fat, 0 g Trans Fat, 32 mg Chol, 84 mg Sod, 19 g Carb, 13 g Sugar, 1 g Fib, 2 g Prot, 13 mg Calc.

4 PointsPlus value

CHOCOLATE-WALNUT BISCOTTI

SERVES 32

1¾ cups whole wheat pastry flour

½ teaspoon baking soda

¼ teaspoon salt

⅓ cup packed brown sugar

⅓ cup granulated sugar

▲ 2 large eggs

1 teaspoon vanilla extract

¾ cup semisweet chocolate chips

¾ cup chopped walnuts

1 Preheat oven to 325°F. Line large baking sheet with parchment paper.

2 Whisk together flour, baking soda, and salt in small bowl. With electric mixer on medium speed, beat brown sugar, granulated sugar, eggs, and vanilla in large bowl until blended. Beat in flour mixture until combined. Stir in chocolate chips and walnuts.

3 Divide dough into three pieces. On floured surface, roll each piece in flour to coat, then shape each into 12-inch log. Transfer logs to prepared baking sheet, placing 3 inches apart. Bake until firm when pressed, about 30 minutes. Cool on baking sheet on rack 15 minutes.

4 Meanwhile, reduce oven temperature to 300°F. Transfer one log at a time to cutting board. With serrated knife, cut into ½-inch-thick diagonal slices, making total of about 64 slices. Stand slices on baking sheet. Bake until dried and crisp, 15–20 minutes. Transfer biscotti to racks to cool completely.

PER SERVING (2 biscotti): 81 Cal, 3 g Total Fat, 1 g Sat Fat, 0 g Trans Fat, 14 mg Chol, 43 mg Sod, 12 g Carb, 7 g Sugar, 1 g Fib, 2 g Prot, 9 mg Calc.

Weekend Treats

FROM TOP, CLOCKWISE:
CHOCOLATE-WALNUT BISCOTTI,
PAGE 239; MOLASSES SPICE
AND RAISIN COOKIES; TRIPLE
CHOCOLATE BROWNIES,
PAGE 238.

MOLASSES SPICE AND RAISIN COOKIES

SERVES 30

¾ **cup all-purpose flour**

½ **cup whole wheat pastry flour**

1 **teaspoon cinnamon**

½ **teaspoon ground ginger**

½ **teaspoon baking powder**

¼ **teaspoon baking soda**

¼ **teaspoon salt**

½ **cup packed dark brown sugar**

¼ **cup light molasses**

3 **tablespoons canola oil**

▲ 2 **tablespoons unsweetened applesauce**

▲ 1 **large egg**

¾ **cup raisins**

1 **cup confectioners' sugar**

1 **tablespoon low-fat (1%) milk**

❶ Preheat oven to 350°F. Line 2 large baking sheets with parchment paper.

❷ Whisk together all-purpose flour, pastry flour, cinnamon, ginger, baking powder, baking soda, and salt in medium bowl. With electric mixer on low speed, beat brown sugar, molasses, oil, applesauce, and egg in large bowl until well blended. Add flour mixture and beat until combined. Stir in raisins. Let batter stand 10 minutes.

❸ Drop batter by heaping teaspoonfuls onto baking sheets, about 2 ½ inches apart, making total of 30 cookies. Bake one sheet at a time, until cookies spring back when pressed, about 10 minutes. Cool on baking sheet 1 minute before transferring with spatula to rack to cool completely.

❹ Stir together confectioners' sugar and milk in small bowl. Place sheet of wax paper under rack. Frost cookies with glaze. Let stand until glaze sets, about 30 minutes.

PER SERVING (1 cookie): 83 Cal, 2 g Total Fat, 0 g Sat Fat, 0 g Trans Fat, 7 mg Chol, 45 mg Sod, 17 g Carb, 13 g Sugar, 1 g Fib, 1 g Prot, 18 mg Calc.

Weekend Treats

Recipes by *PointsPlus* value

2

Angel Food Cupcakes with Marshmallow Frosting, 228

Banana-Coconut Raita, 203

Chocolate-Walnut Biscotti, 239

Green Papaya Salad, 180

Green Salad with Ginger-Carrot Vinaigrette, 132

Miso-Mushroom Soup, 133

Molasses Spice and Raisin Cookies, 241

3

Black-and-White Cupcakes, 226

Ceviche-Style Shrimp Salad with Mango and Avocado, 87

Enlightened Guacamole with Jicama Dipping Sticks, 88

Mango Salad with Lime and Ginger, 204

Mini Bagels with Silky Tofu-Cherry Spread, 23

Mushrooms Stuffed with Sausage and Broccoli Rabe, 63

Sake-Grilled Jumbo Shrimp, 147

Scallion Eggs with Vegetables and Tofu, 151

4

Cherry-Orange Breakfast Scones, 233

Chicken and Vegetable Yakitori, 140

Chicken Tikka Masala, 208

Cod Cioppino, 73

Garlicky Greek Potato Dip (Skordalia), 112

Greek Salad with Feta and Artichokes, 110

Lemongrass Pork Satay with Spicy Cucumber Salad, 185

Lemon-Oregano Grilled Mahimahi and Sweet Onions, 122

Lentil Mulligatawny Soup with Papadams, 202

Morning Carrot-Zucchini Muffins, 232

Mussels Fra Diavolo with Fresh Herbs, 76

Peach Coffee Cake with Crumb Topping, 230

Pork and Mushroom Mu Shu Rolls, 156

Roasted Barbecue Pork with Fresh Kimchi, 187

Rosemary Chicken with Fresh Tomato and Balsamic Sauce, 67

Sesame Tofu and Edamame Stir-Fry, 148

Shrimp and Tomato Curry, 215

Smoked Salmon and Egg White Omelette, 16

Tomato and Okra Stew with Chickpeas, 127

Triple Chocolate Brownies, 238

Vegetable Pad Thai, 197

Whole Wheat Skillet Pancake with Pears and Walnuts, 25

5

Baked Fish and Clams with Cilantro-Mint Sauce, 217

Brown Rice Gomasio with Shiitakes and Tempeh, 150

Chili-Garlic Pork with Bok Choy, 161

Clams with Black Bean Sauce and Fresh Chile, 174

Filet Steaks with Sesame-Wasabi Butter and Watercress, 134

General Tso's Scallops, 170

Grilled Miso-Flavored Eggplants with Adzuki Bean Salad, 149

Hot-and-Sour Soup with Smoked Tofu, 158

Korean Steak Kebabs with Spicy Cilantro Sauce, 182

Negamaki-Style Beef and Green Bean Rolls, 136

Quinoa and Vegetable Risotto, 81

Raspberry-Chocolate Shortbread Bars, 236

Ricotta Pancakes with Berries, 26

Roast Pork Tonnato, 66

Saag Paneer with Peas, 219

Smoked Chicken Waldorf Salad, 50

Souvlaki-Style Pork Chops with Tzatziki, 116

Spicy Chana Masala with Sweet Potato, 218

Spicy Tortellini and Roast Tomato Soup, 49

Streusel-Topped Apple-Buttermilk Muffins, 231

Summer Rolls with Crab and Mango, 181

Turkey Nacho Salad, 51

Turkey Saltimbocca with Lemon and Sage, 72

Turkish Bulgur Pilaf with Vegetables, 126

6

Bahian Fish Stew, 101

Chicken Korma with Cauliflower, 209

Chicken Milanese with Savory Watercress, 68

Cinnamon Rolls with Cream Cheese Frosting, 235

Curried Beef and Mango Wraps, 36

Egg and Asparagus Breakfast Pitas, 19

English Muffin BLT with Avocado, 20

Fruit and Flax Muesli Mix, 31

Goan Chicken Curry, 212

Greek Fishermen's Pot, 124

Grilled Calamari and Orzo Salad, 77

Grilled Chicken Gyros with Bell Pepper, 119

Halibut Teriyaki with Sesame Snow Peas, 144

Hearty Chicken and Soba Noodle Soup, 142

Kung Pao Turkey with Cashews, 166

Loaded Veggie Sandwiches, 44

Moussaka in Minutes, 113

Mushroom and Goat Cheese Quesadillas, 105

Pork and Green Chile Posole Stew, 91

Recipes that work with the Simply Filling technique:

TUNA AND NEW POTATO SALAD WITH BASIL DRESSING, PAGE 55

Index

Note: Page numbers in *italic* type indicate photographs.